TROPICAL *aquarium* FISHES

Fishes of all shapes and colorations can live happily together in the aquarium, occupying all levels of the water

TROPICAL *aquarium* FISHES

DICK MILLS

WHSMITH
EXCLUSIVE
· BOOKS ·

This edition produced exclusively for
W H Smith

Published by
The Hamlyn Publishing Group Limited
a division of The Octopus Publishing Group plc
Michelin House, 81 Fulham Road
London SW3 6RB

ISBN 0 600 56052 X

Printed by Mandarin Offset in Hong Kong

Contents

Introduction

The attraction of a well-established aquarium is undeniable as one watches shoals of beautifully-coloured fishes weaving gracefully through luxuriant underwater vegetation. The beginner is naturally anxious to achieve a similar effect as soon as possible. An aquarium is, however, a living system which takes some time to mature, so a little patience is one of the first requirements for the novice fishkeeper. On the other hand, the technical aspects of aquarium management such as heating, lighting etc. are now easy to control thanks to reliable and efficient modern equipment.

Before choosing which fishes to keep consider how large an aquarium you can realistically accommodate and how much time and money you wish to devote to your hobby. A fine display of small, spectacular and easy-to-keep species can be achieved for a modest outlay in space, time and cash. More demanding, if less decorative, species may attract the more scientifically-minded hobbyist who wishes to study the behaviour of a single species or group more closely. In this case you could consider recreating their natural habitat in your aquarium. Those interested in fish breeding might find the livebearing fishes of particular interest, where a disciplined breeding programme can produce a new strain of a particular colour or fin shape.

Fish come in many shapes, sizes and colours. There is a vast range of species available for the freshwater aquarium (see the illustrated section for descriptions of individual species and their requirements). Faced with this choice where do you start? The primitive law of survival should be applied first. Big fish will eat little fish so do not be tempted to mix extremes of sizes. Some fish are more boisterous than others; slow-moving fishes, often with elongated, graceful fins, will not appreciate the constant darting about of more lively fishes. Small fishes will certainly be intimidated by any faster-moving larger fish, whether it intends to eat them or not.

Many fish have a natural timetable of activity that does not fit in with their owner's. Not all will display themselves at your convenience just because you have switched on the aquarium light and settled down to watch them. Many worthwhile species are nocturnal or naturally shy, and you may have to use trickery to tempt them out (see page 15).

Plan the best use of the aquarium's swimming space. Different types of fish swim and feed at different levels in the tank. Some are surface-feeders, some feed exclusively on the bottom and some prefer to stay in midwater. By including fishes of each type you can stock the space available to the best advantage. A rough guide to which of these groups a fish belongs is the position of the mouth. Surface-feeders have a mouth situated towards the top of the head, bottom-feeders have a definitely underslung mouth, usually with barbels around it and a flat underside to the body. A mouth located right at the tip of the snout of a symmetrically-shaped fish usually indicates a midwater feeder.

The environment you create for your fish with gravel, rocks and underwater vegetation is as important as the fish themselves, both for their well-being and your enjoyment. Once you have decided which fish to keep, the aquarium conditions can be tailored to their requirements. (Fishkeepers who are also plant lovers may wish to steer clear of some herbivorous species which quickly reduce any vegetation to a few stalks in as many minutes!)

Once hooked, one aquarium may soon not seem enough. But, for the fishes' sake, make haste slowly. Your fish cannot swim away from your neglect – they depend on you for their survival. Your own pleasure will be in direct proportion to your skill in looking after the fish in the manner they undoubtedly deserve. Give them the best care and they will repay you with the best display.

Providing the *Correct Living* Conditions

Faced with the wide range of fishes from an equally wide range of sources, the beginner may wonder how all their requirements can be satisfied in one aquarium. But most of the commonly-available fish are relatively hardy individuals and can tolerate some degree of change. In their natural habitat they have to adapt to seasonal changes as a matter of course. It is unlikely that you will be attempting to keep the more difficult fishes at the outset as they can be expensive and hard to find in the shops.

A fish's requirements can be broken down into separate manageable segments. Basically it needs **space**, **security**, **heat**, **light** and, of course, **water.** (Feeding and health are covered in a later chapter.) In nature, **cleanliness** is taken care of by water movements, wind, rain and the fish's ability to swim away from poor conditions. In the aquarium you must attend to this requirement by regular routine maintenance of the tank and its associated equipment.

*Red Swordtails (*Xiphophorus helleri*) are prolific, active livebearing fishes*

SPACE

A roomy aquarium will not only present the best display to you the viewer but is necessary for many other reasons. Fish cannot always be treated as individuals; many are gregarious by nature and if kept singly (even if they are with other species in a well-stocked tank) they may not thrive in captivity. Such species are best kept in shoals of at least a dozen so that they display their normal way of life to you. At the other extreme, fishes can become very territorially-minded, especially at breeding time, and unless the aquarium is roomy enough to give such fish their own personal territory they will not breed and may fight with fish on adjacent territories. There is a further good reason for selecting a good-sized aquarium: conditions in a large body of water tend to remain more stable than those in a smaller volume. However, choosing a big tank is only part of the story.

Fish breathe oxygen dissolved in the water and, like other animals, breathe out carbon dioxide. The only way the oxygen in the water can be replenished is through the water surface (this is also one of the places where unwanted carbon dioxide can be expelled from the aquarium, but there are other ways of removing this gas, as we shall see later). If you consider two tanks of identical volume but different shape, fishes in them will have the same space in which to swim, but in the tank of the more horizontal design there is more surface and bottom *area* for both territorial purposes and for gaseous exchange at the water surface.

How many fish will any tank hold? As a rough guide, tropical fish need about 30 cm^2 of water surface area per centimetre of body length (approx. 13 sq. in per inch body length) (do not include the tail in length measurement). An aquarium measuring 60 cm (24 in) long by 30 cm (12 in) front to back has a water surface area of 1800 cm^2 (60×30) (288 sq. in) and will comfortably support 60 cm (24 in) of fish length. This guideline has to be interpreted sensibly – putting a single fish of the 'allowed' total 60 cm length into a tank itself only 60 cm long would not be exactly practical. On a more serious note, bigger fishes use up more oxygen than smaller ones so opting for smaller fishes is safer, and also provides you with a better display.

Modern aquariums come in standard sizes: lengths are usually in 30 cm (12 in) multiples, widths are also around 30 or 38 cm (12 or 15 in), as are the water depth dimensions. Such tanks are all-glass: five pieces of glass being glued together with silicone sealant acting as a firm adhesive. You are not irrevocably bound to such dimensioned tanks. Their construction is so simple that you can custom-build a tank to any required size or shape; there are many deviations from the normal oblong box design – a hexagonal free-standing 'island' tank is quite attractive.

Tanks need no longer look ugly, and many designs are available where the tank is incorporated into a piece of furniture – bookshelves and cabinets are favourite basic designs, where the shelves and cupboard space can be used to house the aquarium equipment neatly and unobtrusively. You can have a tank exactly to suit your requirements, but a word of warning: very cheap tanks may be made from thin glass which may not be able to stand up to the high pressure exerted on it by a large volume of water.

SECURITY and GENERAL ENVIRONMENT

What could be more secure, you may ask, than a fish in a home aquarium? It is in no danger from predators (except cats) nor from threats to its well-being (apart from inquisitive small fingers turning off the electricity). But fish do need security in the aquarium if they are to feel completely at home.

In the main we furnish the aquarium to suit ourselves, deliberately providing open space and expecting the fish to swim just where we can see them. We have the tank lights blazing a permanent sunshine down on them. To the fish there seems no respite to being constantly on show.

There is a way of providing security for the fishes and yet to fulfill our need to have something beautiful to look at at the same time – rockwork and aquarium plants.

Rockwork

It is easy to create caves and terraces using pieces of aquarium-suitable rock stuck together with aquarium sealant. You can make an entire background for the rear wall and two sides of the aquarium using this method, but you must make sure that there is no way a fish can get behind it and die unnoticed. Sticking rocks directly on to the glass is one way but then you cannot change your mind later. Creating underwater cliffs is one way of adding interest to the tank, especially if the fish you intend keeping are not only cave-dwellers but plant-eaters too. Another reason for making hiding places is to provide spawning sites for the more secretive species, many of which lay eggs upside down on the ceiling of a cave.

Anything you put into the tank will affect the water quality (see page 15). Soluble rocks and gravel should not be used, nor should any containing visible signs of metal ores. Any calcium in the rocks or gravel will gradually harden the water over a period of time and calcium-free gravel is available for use where soft water conditions are to be maintained. Suitable non-soluble rocks include slate, granite and basalt. Branches of wood are also safe as long as they are long-dead and do not release acids and tannins into the water – boiling the wood followed by soaking it for long periods in changes of fresh water, or sealing with polyurethane paint, usually renders it safe for aquarium use. Artificial moulded-resin 'logs' are quite safe to use.

Plants

Plants provide many services to the aquarium. They create shade and hiding places, offering convenient safe retreats when danger threatens or when a fish simply wants to get away from it all. Plants also play a major part in keeping the aquarium clean (see page 14).

Many fish make practical use of plants. The soft-leaved species make good eating for herbivorous fishes whilst the firmer, stout-leaved plants offer favourable spawning aids – either as spawning sites themselves or as nest-building materials.

As far as the hobbyist is concerned a primary use for plants is as aquarium decorations, and here they can be used with great imagination and artistic skill. Aquarium plants may be divided into three groups – floating plants, rooted plants and bunched plants. As their name suggests, floating plants are not anchored in the gravel base but remain on the water surface; most have trailing roots which hang down in the water, absorbing nutrients and providing sanctuary for young fishes. The main group, rooted plants, make up the decorative species and contain both fine- and broad-leaved species. Bunched plants are rapid-growing species from which regular cuttings may be taken to be re-rooted in the gravel to provide extra stocks. The following list gives some suitable aquarium plants and their particular uses.

Floating species

Azolla caroliniana, Fairy Moss, is a tiny fern. The leaves are red or green but often appear greyish due to the tiny hairs on their surface. Quite decorative but not of great practical importance as far as the fishes are concerned.

Ceratophyllum submersum, Hornwort, is a cosmopolitan plant with hard bristly whorls of leaves. It is a tropical version of the coldwater species *C.demersum* and it prefers to grow as a tangled mass rather than be rooted down. The brittle leaves send out rootlets very readily.

Lemna minor, Lesser Duckweed, can become a curse in the aquarium. Although its tiny oval leaves bring welcome shade, they spread with alarming haste to cover the entire water surface if unchecked. Some large Barbs relish them as food so netfuls can be removed regularly to good effect.

Najas microdon, is a much-branched brittle plant with narrow leaves. Left to its own devices it develops into a tangled mass in mid-water where it is useful as a spawning medium for egglayers and a sanctuary for fry. Also known as *N.guadalupensis*.

Pistia stratiotes, Water Lettuce, resembles a floating lettuce except that the pale green leaves are velvety, being covered in tiny hairs. When large, the

Java Moss

Crystalwort, Riccia

Fairy Moss

Eel Grass, Tape Grass, *Vallisneria*

leaves may easily become scorched by the aquarium lamps or damaged by condensation droplets, but the long trailing roots make very good retreats for young fry.

Riccia fluitans, Crystalwort, hangs just below the surface, a mass of tiny bright green ribbons which constantly branch out spreading through the water. Used as bubblenest building material.

Salvinia auriculata, Butterfly Fern, is similar in many ways to Duckweed: its hairy leaves are oval-shaped, but larger, and it can be just as rampant. May be used for bubblenest building.

Rooted species

Aponogeton spp. do not have conventional roots but emerge from a rhizome or tuberous growth. Many are very beautiful, their leaves having ruffled edges or appearing lace-like where the tissue between the leaf veins is entirely absent. They bear flowers above water; pollinating these with a soft brush (or even brushing two flowers together) results in seeds being set which can be sown in shallow water to produce new plants. Requires a winter rest period in cooler water.

Ceratopteris thalictroides, Indian Fern, is a fast-growing, pale green plant with indented leaves not unlike Water Wistaria. May grow rooted in the gravel but often floats upwards under its own buoyancy. Daughter plants emerge on individual leaves of parent plant.

Cryptocoryne spp. make up a large family of very decorative aquarium plants. Leaf shapes can be narrow or broad depending on species and arise from a central rosette. Sizes vary from tiny, gravel-carpeting species to huge 'wedding bouquet' proportions. Most are quite happy to flourish in subdued lighting and the larger-leaved species make ideal spawning sites for Angelfish.

Eleocharis acicularis, Hair-grass, cannot be mistaken for any other plant. The very narrow leaves are tubular and rise in groups from the root system. It looks particularly effective when planted in front of a large piece of rock.

Hygrophila spp. are quick-growing woody plants ideal for filling spaces and corners in the aquarium. Leaves are pointed and oval, occurring in opposite pairs on a single stem. Ready rooters, they provide plenty of cuttings. *H.difformis*, Water Wisteria, also known as *Synnema triflorum*, has highly-indented leaves.

Sagittaria spp. are old aquarium favourites. Leaves are strap-shaped and the plant is ideal for use as a background around the back and sides of the tank. Varieties of different sizes are available from low gravel coverers to very large, water surface trailing types. It reproduces by young plants developing from vegetative runners although flowers may also be seen under aquarium conditions.

Vallisneria spp. are very similar in appearance to *Sagittaria* and can be used to the same effect. A favourite and very decorative variety, *V.tortifolia*, has tightly-spiralled leaves.

Vesicularia dubyana, Java Moss, is an excellent spawning medium for egg-laying fishes. The tiny leaves provide a dense 'egg-trap' as the spawning fish dive into it. Like coldwater Willow Moss it attaches itself to any firm surface by means of tiny rambling roots.

Bunched species

Cabomba caroliniana, Carolinian Fanwort, is a favourite amongst hobbyists, especially with those who find it no problem to grow. Its fine whorls of leaves need very clean water if they are not to become clogged with detritus. Bright light is also necessary for successful growth.

Egeria densa, Giant 'Elodea', has three or four leaves which curl back from a central stem at close intervals. A rapidly-growing plant which provides many cuttings which, in turn, send down rootlets to the gravel.

Myriophyllum hippuroides, Water Milfoil, is another fine-leaved plant similar to *Cabomba* and requiring the same care, especially clean water and prevention of clogging by algae.

Indian Water Star (*Hygrophila polysperma*)
Water Wisteria
Carolinian Fanwort (*Cambomba carolinana*)
Butterfly Fern
Indian Fern (submerged type)
Indian Fern (floating type)
Giant 'Elodea'
Aponogeton ulvaceus
Water Milfoil
Cryptocoryne willisii
Hair-grass

HEAT

Beginners often worry about maintaining the necessary warmth in the aquarium. The water temperature required is 25°C (77°F). This is only slightly warm, and is not too expensive to maintain, once the total volume of water has reached the desired temperature.

Heating equipment for the aquarium is basically an electric heating coil, complete with thermostat to control it, both contained in a glass tube. This is submerged in the aquarium, connected to the electricity supply, switched on and that is all there is to it. An in-built neon indicator will tell you that it is functioning correctly. You should also have a thermometer in the aquarium to monitor the temperature. There are various designs of heating equipment; it is possible to have a separate thermostat and heater. Thermostats can also be placed inside the tank (submersibles) or externally (fixed to the wall of the aquarium). They may be of electro-mechanical design or use solid-state microchip circuitry. Heaters are available in standard sizes, usually rated in 50 watt (electrical consumption) multiples. A guide to the correct size of heater for your aquarium is to allow 2 watts per litre (~9 watts per gallon) of water capacity for standard tanks of 60 cm (24 in) length; larger tanks (which lose heat more slowly) can use heaters of a slightly lower wattage/litre rating.

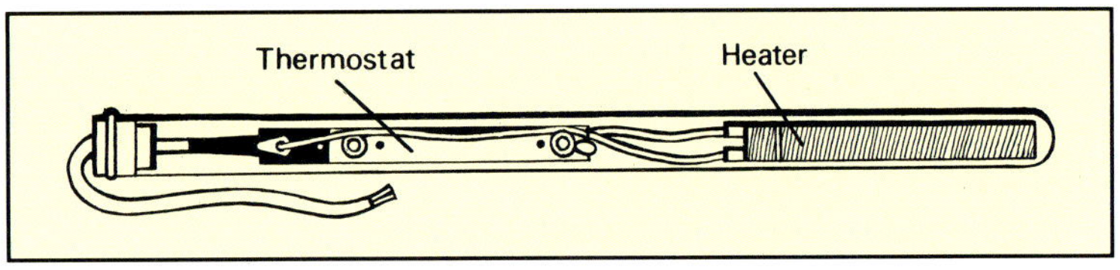

Recent freshwater aquarium development has seen the incorporation of heating equipment in the body of an external power filter, and the introduction of external heating mats that go under the tank itself.

Exact, degree-accuracy control of water temperature is not necessary – even in the tropics water temperatures vary according to time of day or night. Control of temperature can be useful, however, during breeding, when a slight rise (or even fall) may trigger the breeding urge.

LIGHT

Light is important in the aquarium for it provides the stimulus for activity both for fishes and plants. (Another important factor is that it also lets you see the fish!)

Plants require light in order to *photosynthesize*, that is, to build up stocks of food within their cells for growth. A vital part of this process helps to maintain good water conditions, as a necessary ingredient for photosynthesis is carbon dioxide. All the time the aquarium receives light, the plants take up carbon dioxide from the water and, even better, give off oxygen. (At night this process is reversed, the plants using up oxygen and giving off carbon dioxide.)

The most convenient way of lighting the aquarium is to use fluorescent lamps. These are far better than tungsten types (bulbs) for they give off an even light, produce much less heat and are less costly to run. Available in lengths of 30 cm (12 in) multiples, they can be obtained in various 'colours'. White or 'Northlight' tubes may look too 'cold' or render the fishes' colours incorrectly. Tubes designed for horticultural use have an increase in output of their red/orange and blue/violet wavelengths and whilst these are beneficial to plants they can exaggerate the colours of the fish. Warm white tubes, and those closely approximating to natural sunlight, provide the most acceptable light, but any combination can be used to suit individual tastes.

The trick with lighting is to get the amount just right – too little and the plants will not grow, too much and they get smothered in green algae. Tropical plants are used to bright light for around 12 hours each day. A rough starting guide is to allow 20 watts per 30 cm (12 in) length of tank: again, referring to our 60 (24 in) long tank, some 40 watts of tube lighting will be needed. You may be lucky and find that 2 × 20 watt tubes fit nicely into the tank hood, otherwise some compromise must be found using three slightly smaller tubes overlapped where necessary. The final amount/intensity of light required can only be found by trial and error – to avoid algal growth try planting more plants, these will crowd out the alga by denying it vital light.

For large, deep tanks more powerful lamps will be needed to get light to the bottom. Metal halide and mercury vapour lamps are useful but are more expensive than fluorescent tubes and also require mounting some distance above water level, which means doing away with the normal aquarium hood/reflector.

Whatever lamps you use must be protected against spray, condensation and water damage. Use waterproofed fittings and always use a cover-glass on top of the aquarium before fitting the hood. These measures will protect the lamps but keep the cover-glass spotlessly clean to let the precious light through.

Some nocturnal fish have to be tempted out by trickery. Try keeping tank lights bright when you are not around and *reducing* lighting levels when you want to look at the fish. This may persuade them that night has fallen and it is time to come out.

Most water tests involve a comparison of colours between the mixture of the water to be tested and reagent and the standard colour chart, in this case provided in the form of a colour gel wheel

WATER

The phrase 'like a fish out of water' reminds us of the importance of the liquid that supports all aquatic life. Water quality can vary from place to place and differences in composition can be important when keeping fish.

Water is quite pure when it first forms as rain, but by the time it reaches the ground has usually absorbed substances on the way down. Industrial effluent in the atmosphere can turn water to a weak acid, and the nature of the ground on which it falls can have a further effect. Fishes also have differing water requirements – some come from well-oxygenated, fast-flowing mountain streams, some from shallow jungle waters with rotting vegetation, and some from slow-running muddy rivers and motionless lakes and ponds.

Basic water quality can be measured in two main ways – whether it is acid or alkaline, and whether it is hard or soft. Inexpensive test kits are available to ascertain the water's exact quality – pH kits (to measure acidity/alkalinity) and hardness kits. Other test kits can be used to measure the levels of individual substances such as nitrite, nitrate and copper, but the use of these is beyond the scope of this book. The beginner need not be too preoccupied with these factors (a rough guide is that soft waters tend to be acid, hard waters alkaline), but should appreciate the risks the fish are exposed to when faced with a change from one type of water to another. Fish caught in the wild or bred in commercial fish-farms will certainly not be accustomed to the water emerging from our domestic supply, which has been treated to render it safe for human consumption but not necessarily ideal for fish keeping.

This modern reflector hood has provision for fitting either type of lighting – fluorescent tube or tungsten bulbs

Most of the fishes available from your dealer will be hardy enough to keep in domestic tapwater, providing that some safeguards are taken. Exposure to fresh chlorine-treated tapwater is bad for the fish (even if the temperature is correct) so before using water in the aquarium it should be treated with a proprietary water conditioner which will not only neutralize the chlorine and precipitate harmful metals, but also protect the fish's delicate gill membranes. Water from a copper-piped hot water system should not be used, as copper is very toxic to fish; draw water straight from the mains supply, treat it with the appropriate water conditioner and aerate it thoroughly before use.

It is good policy to find out from your dealer, in advance of buying fish, whether or not they are being kept in any particular water conditions, so that you can adjust your own aquarium conditions to suit. If the dealer is local, then it is more than likely that fish from him will thrive in your tapwater too. Most fish do best in slightly soft acid water, but two major exceptions to this are livebearing fishes and fishes from the African Rift Valley lakes; both these groups of fishes appreciate harder water.

The question of absolute water quality becomes more important when breeding, especially when attempting the more 'difficult' species. Here, the creation and maintenance of special water conditions (closely approximating those found in nature) may be necessary not only to stimulate the fishes to breed but also for the successful development of the eggs into fry.

The simple internal box filter draws aquarium water down through the filter medium then expels the clean water out at the top. You must clean the filter medium regularly – it is all too easy to forget the filter is there once the aquarium plants have fully developed

CLEANLINESS

Water in nature is kept clean by the action of wind, rain and water currents. In the aquarium the water is virtually static and waste products from the fishes together with dead and decaying plant material build up.

Aeration

Getting rid of carbon dioxide is an important task and plants can help, but by artificially aerating the water using airpumps and airstones (see Setting up the aquarium) we can create a physical turnover of the water, exposing the lower levels to the air, venting off the carbon dioxide and assisting replenishment of oxygen.

Water changes

One simple way of keeping the water relatively clean is by making partial water changes. Siphoning off water from near the bottom of the tank takes sediment with it, and adding fresh water dilutes the amount of dissolved wastes at the same time. Changing about 20 per cent of the water every 2 to 3 weeks is normal practice.

Filtration systems

Another way is to employ some form of filtration system. These vary both in complexity and in their method of dealing with waste. The simplest form of filtration entails passing the aquarium water through a box containing fibrous material (use a man-made fibre such as Dacron rather than glass-fibre) which strains out any suspended matter; this cannot remove dissolved waste products which are removed by activated carbon, a substance with a very large surface area on which the dissolved wastes are adsorbed. These basic filters can either be placed in the water inside the aquarium or hung on the aquarium side, where the water is driven through them using air from the aquarium airpump. More sophisticated designs employ small electrically-driven pumps

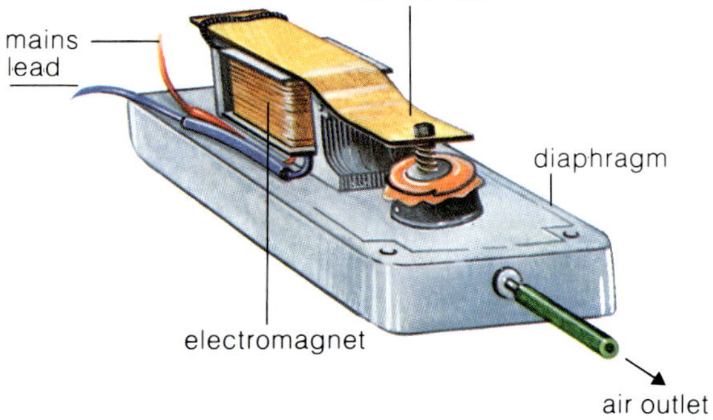

The internal workings of a vibrator diaphragm airpump. Always disconnect the power supply first before removing the cover

to increase the waterflow (and thus the filter efficiency) through the filter. The tiniest particles can be removed from the water and one type of filter that uses diatomaceous earth as the filter medium removes particles down to 1 μm in size, which makes it possible to remove disease-carrying organisms and parasites. After this ultra-fine straining process the water is extremely clear.

Choose a filter that will turn over the water in the aquarium two or three times an hour; although filters have their flow rates clearly indicated on the packaging, these rates are based on an *empty* filter. When the filter medium is added the flow rate will be decreased somewhat – even more so as the filter becomes clogged with removed dirt. Allow for this fact when selecting a filter to avoid disappointment in performance.

The forms of filtration described thus far work by mechanical or chemical means. A third form uses bacteria and is termed biological filtration. It is used in association with undergravel filter systems. Bacterial action on waste products in the aquarium produces ammonia, a highly toxic substance. Two further types of bacteria (*Nitrosomonas* and *Nitrobacter*) progressively turn the ammonia into less toxic nitrite and eventually into even safer nitrate. Marshalling these bacteria into action is simple: a perforated or slotted plate is placed on the tank base before the gravel is added and an airline (or electric pump) is added to a vertical tube. Oxygen-carrying water is therefore drawn through the gravel and this supports bacterial life which colonizes the entire gravel bed. As long as the water flow is continuous, the bacteria continue to thrive and do their job. This bacterial colony takes several weeks to become fully established and can be easily overloaded by adding too many fish at once to the system. It is important that fish stocks are built up slowly so that the bacteria can gradually adjust to the increasing waste-product load. Ammonia-based compounds can be removed by other methods, and the necessary ammonia-absorbing materials can be used in mechanical filtration systems. Such materials (usually zeolite) are reusable after recharging by immersion in a salt solution for a few hours.

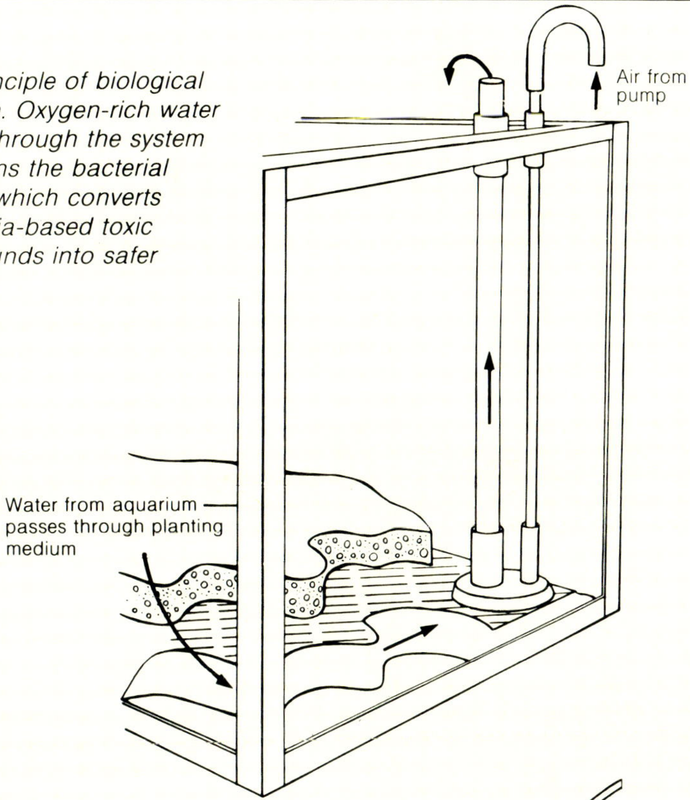

The principle of biological filtration. Oxygen-rich water drawn through the system maintains the bacterial colony which converts ammonia-based toxic compounds into safer nitrates

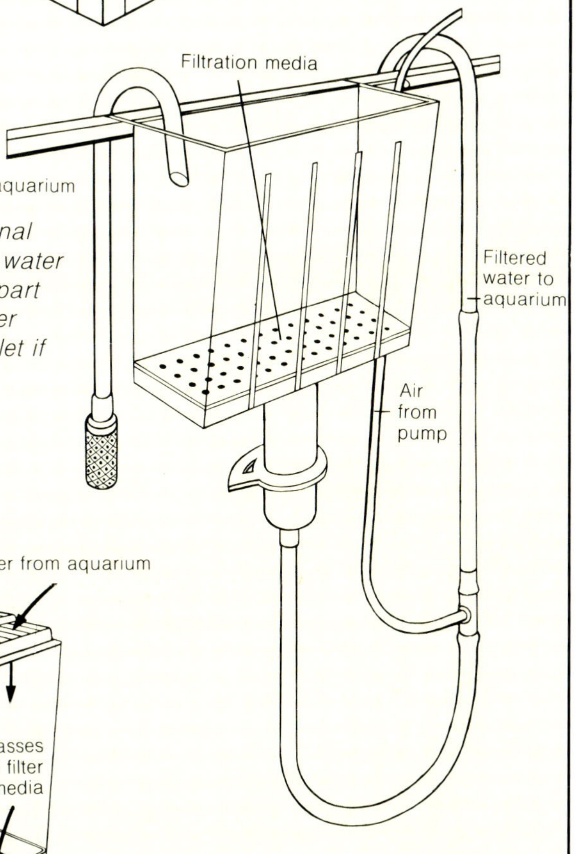

With this type of external box filter, the cleaned water can be returned to a part of the aquarium further away from the filter inlet if so desired

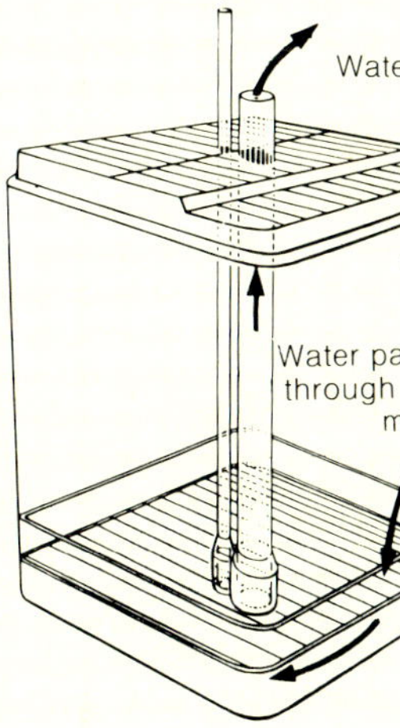

Simple internal box filters are better suited to fry-raising tanks, as they are apt to get neglected in fully-furnished aquariums

Left: The long handle on this simple algae-scraper enables the scraper blade to reach all parts of the front glass

Below: The magnetic types of algae-scraper keeps your hands dry – simply move the outer half, the inside part will follow it scraping off the algae as it goes

Right: Snails may be inadvertently introduced into the aquarium as eggs on plant leaves

Left: Three common aquatic snails: Red Ramshorn snails (1),* Planorbis, *may damage soft-leaved plants;* Bulinus *(2) is an Australian species; whilst the Malayan Sand snail (3),* Thiara, *burrows continuously through the substrate*

Filtration equipment of all types is readily available, and you can easily update the system according to your needs. At the top end of the scale you can buy a fully-integrated filtration system built into the aquarium itself. These systems take the biological filtration process a stage further, having special trickle-filter units which turn nitrate into free atmospheric nitrogen again thus completely ridding the aquarium of any toxic compounds. One final tip for clean conditions – do not overfeed!

KEEPING UP THE GOOD WORK

Even modern equipment depends on you for regular maintenance to enable it to operate at peak efficiency. You should also carry out regular aquarium management checks in order to ensure everything is progressing satisfactorily.

Temperature checks become automatic after a few weeks with a new aquarium, and you can soon, with experience, judge the warmth of the tank glass on your hand. If your aquarium is of a reasonable size, heat losses in the event of heater failure or a power cut will be slow. Lagging the tank with several layers of newspapers or a blanket will help to conserve heat if winter conditions prevail and the power failure is expected to persist for some hours. Standing bottles of hot water in the tank will help to keep temperatures up but be careful the bottles' displacement does not cause the tank to overflow.

PLEASE NOTE: ALWAYS SWITCH OFF THE POWER SUPPLY BEFORE REPLACING, ADJUSTING OR OTHERWISE MAINTAINING ELECTRICALLY-POWERED AQUARIUM EQUIPMENT

Always investigate absentees at feeding time – they might have died, become trapped behind a rock or even jumped out of the tank! Undiscovered fatalities in the tank can lead to pollution and perhaps the spread of disease.

Filter media require periodic cleaning and replacement; filter-floss can often be rinsed clean and reused but activated carbon has a limited life and must be renewed. The usual sign that a filter needs cleaning is a falling-off of water-flow. Neglecting to clean a filter can result in toxic wastes being redissolved back into the aquarium water.

One filter that is often neglected is the small felt pad situated underneath most airpumps. It does an important job of filtering the air before it enters the aquarium, so do not forget to remove it and wash it clean from time to time.

Partial water changes should still be carried out, despite the use of an efficient filtration system, as this will help keep the water chemistry parameters within a narrow range. Siphoning off water from the bottom areas of the tank has already been discussed, and it is also a good idea to fit a wide bore tube on the end of the siphon so that the gravel can be gently siphoned too, any embedded detritus being easily removed without taking gravel with it. Commercially-available 'gravel washers' can be found at your dealer.

By controlling the amount of light accurately, growths of algae should be kept to a manageable minimum. Any that grows on the inside of the front glass can be removed with a steel-wool pad (not soap-filled) or an abrasive magnetic scraper, another very useful aquarium accessory. Do not 'park' magnetic aquarium scrapers near the heater/thermostat as their magnetic fields may interfere with its operation. Do not bother to remove algae growing on the other glass panels, browsing vegetarian fishes will soon dispose of it. Maintenance of lighting equipment is important for optimum plant growth. Fluorescent lamps gradually fall off in performance and usually require changing every six months to a year. Keeping cover-glasses clean and the water clear will allow the plants to make best use of the aquarium lighting.

Remove dead leaves from plants and regularly prune strong-growing species. Cuttings taken in pruning can be re-rooted in the gravel to provide you with increased plant stocks.

All the above chores take, in total, no more than a few minutes each day, perhaps an hour or two every month. Taken in proportion to the time you will spend in front of the aquarium gazing at the activity, this is a very small price to pay for the promise of such marvellous enjoyment.

Setting Up *the* *Aquarium*

Setting up your aquarium should be an enjoyable experience. A little 'forward planning' makes all the difference. You should bear in mind, too, that the aim is not only to provide the fishes with their required conditions but that the aquarium can also be easily serviced. This is so that these carefully prepared conditions can be maintained in the future without any major 'break-down' of the tank being needed. If you are a newcomer to fishkeeping make sure, before you start, that you clearly understand how the various pieces of equipment work and how they fit together: this is particularly necessary with the filtration equipment – halfway through setting-up is no time to realise you have not read the manufacturer's instructions.

On a serious note, with the exception of the airpump, do not be tempted to connect up any electrically-powered equipment to the supply just 'to see if it works': *all* aquarium equipment is meant to operate either with water surrounding it or flowing through it. Electric motors will rapidly overheat if run 'dry' away from the cooling effect of water. Similarly, aquarium heaters will heat up extremely fast out of water and easily cause burns: dropping them into water to cool them down may even result in an explosion.

Never place your hands in the aquarium, or make adjustments to any electrically-powered equipment, unless the electrical supply is switched off.

The following outline of the aquarium setting-up procedure includes details of fitting of several different types of filtration equipment: you will need to decide which one of these is applicable to your own installation plans.

The Neon Tetra, Paracheirodon innesi, *has been a firm favourite with fishkeepers for over 50 years*

SITING

The actual siting of the aquarium, whilst not absolutely critical, can have some effect on its satisfactory operation and continuing success.

A fully-stocked aquarium is heavy, so a firm, level base must be chosen. Although aquariums make ideal additions for flat-dwellers the weight of the aquarium on an upstairs floor must not be underestimated. Make sure the weight is distributed evenly, preferably sharing the load over floor joists. A window location is not suitable: daylight is uncontrollable and too much direct sun will overheat the tank and produce extra algal growth. Siting the aquarium near a power outlet socket is a distinct advantage as trailing wires can be a safety hazard – especially with water around. An alcove out of direct sunlight is ideal – here, the aquarium environment, free from outside influences and cold draughts, can be completely controlled.

YOU WILL NEED:

Aquarium with its cover-glass and hood
Heater/thermostat unit(s)
Lights
Filtration system (mechanical, chemical or biological)
Airpump, airline and airstones
Cable tidy
Rockwork
Gravel (and any additional base covering material)
Plants
Suitably-treated water – *not* chlorinated water straight from the tap.
Sealant, scissors, pliers, screwdriver
An electric plug!

ASSEMBLY

Before you start, place all the things you will need within easy reach, not only the 'ingredients' for the aquarium itself but also scissors, pliers etc. Before setting up, test the tank for leaks (outdoors), and wash the gravel and rocks. If you intend making up rocky structures as tank decorations these can be made in advance. Plants should be rinsed and inspected for snails' eggs and other unwanted passengers before being divided into their various species groups: keep them between sheets of wet newspaper whilst awaiting planting.

For the sake of safety and tidiness it is a good idea to use a 'cable tidy' switched control box for all aquarium electrical connections; these are available from your dealer and are simple to use. The lights and pump are connected to the switched terminals, whilst heating circuits are normally unswitched. Mount the cable tidy on the end of the tank nearest the power supply socket.

All-glass aquariums should have an absorbent cushion beneath them to iron out any unevenness in the surface on which the tank will stand. A sheet of expanded polystyrene (styrofoam) cut to the dimensions of the tank base is ideal.

If biological filtration is to be used, the filter plate must be put into the tank before the base-covering gravel is added. Make sure that the filter plate is well bedded down and covers the whole

These various components all go together to form the complete aquarium

base; failure to do this will result in water finding its way around the plate instead of going through the gravel, and if the plate does not cover the whole base some areas will become stagnant and anaerobic (lacking oxygen). Fit the vertical tube to the filter plate now otherwise gravel will get into the hole later. If a motorized powerhead is to be used, do not fit it at this stage as it may topple off as you continue to work within the aquarium, with dire results.

Put large rocks directly on to the filter plate or the tank base. In this way they will be supported by the rest of the gravel and be less likely to topple.

Spread washed gravel over the filter plate (if fitted) or directly on the tank base to a depth of 2–3 cm (1–1½ in). If digging fishes are to be kept, it is a good idea to use a 'gravel tidy'. This is a piece of perforated plastic sheeting which is laid on the gravel before the final layers are added. Its purpose is to stop fishes digging down too far and exposing the biological filter plate. Add the rest of the gravel and slope it so that it rises a further 5–7 cm (2–3 in) at the rear of the tank; this gives a good visual aspect when viewed from the front and also means that any dirt will collect at a convenient area from where it can be siphoned off quite easily.

It is best to fit the aquarium hardware before access to the aquarium becomes limited by the presence of rockwork or plants. Fit the heater/thermostat combined unit to the rear wall of the tank, long models are best mounted diagonally. Connect the wiring to the appropriate cable tidy terminal block but do *not* connect the mains supply to the cable tidy yet.

Hang external filter boxes on the rear or side of the tank and fill them with filter medium. Similarly fill internal filter boxes (add a few small pebbles too to weight them down) and place them in position at the rear of the aquarium.

Airvalves, which control the airflow from the airpump to airstones and air-operated filters, are best ganged together in a block in one convenient place, usually stuck to the side of the aquarium in a similar manner to the cable tidy. Connect one end of a length of airline to an airstone and its other end to an outlet on the block. Connect another airline from the airlift tube of the internal/external filter box (or undergravel filter) to another outlet.

In the airline from pump to inlet connection on the airvalve block insert a one-way, non-return valve; this will prevent water siphoning back from the tank and damaging the airpump. Connect the airpump wire to the cable tidy block at the appropriate terminals.

Like the airpump, power filters can stand alongside the aquarium or be placed on a convenient shelf beneath it. Connect the 'fish-guard' to the inlet siphon tube and connect this tube to the inlet pipe on the filter; retain in position with suction pads if necessary. Connect one end of the return pipe to the waterpump outlet and its other end to a spraybar fixed, in turn, by suction pads to the rear wall of the aquarium. Make sure that the holes in the spraybar are pointing *downwards* and that all hose fixings are securely tightened. Fill the canister body with suitable filter medium. Again, as with all electrical equipment, do not connect to the mains supply yet.

Returning to the tank decorations, hide the hardware and pipework with strategically-placed rockwork but do not obstruct waterflow to the filter's inlet tube. View the set-up frequently through the front glass to check satisfactory artistic progress.

It is now time to fill the tank with water. This should be done gently to avoid disturbing the contoured gravel. Using a hose let water first flow into a saucer or small jug placed on the gravel – the overflow will fill the tank without disturbance. When the tank has only a few centimetres left to fill, stop the water supply. Now is the best moment to plant the tank: the plants will take up their natural positions in the water and you will be able to judge the effect instantly.

The final fully-furnished aquarium should be both beautiful and functional

Plant the back and sides of the tank first with tall species such as *Vallisneria* and *Sagittaria*. Rooted plants should be placed in holes in the gravel, spreading the roots with the fingers: the junction between plant leaf or stem and the root system should be just clear of the gravel surface. Working towards the middle and front of the tank, add bushy species to fill in corners, and the larger specimen plants to best effect. Do not be too sparing with plants, it is quite common to have 50 plants per square foot (900 cm^2). Once planting is complete, fill the tank completely and add any floating plants. Finally, do not forget to install the powerhead to the undergravel lift tube, and wire it to the cable tidy.

Prime external filter boxes by submerging the siphon tube in water, sealing with fingers (or filter starting stick cap) and releasing when the top end of siphon is over the filter box but *below the level of water in the tank*. The water level in the filter box will rise, automatically stopping when the level is the same as that in the main tank. Power filter bodies are primed by sucking at the end of the outlet pipe after first disconnecting the return pipe; when water emerges reconnect the pipe.

Fit cover-glasses – two half-size cover-glasses make for easier feeding – and install lamps in the reflector hood. The starter gear for fluorescent lamps is heavy and should only be mounted on the hood with care, otherwise mount in any convenient position near to the tank and wire it to the cable tidy control block. Finally fit a plug to the cable tidy mains supply wire and attach to mains power outlet and switch on.

The aquarium lights should come on, bubbles emerge from airstones, water from filter returns and the neon indicator on the thermostat unit should glow. (If only one or two things work, check that the switches on the cable tidy are not in the off position.) If the airpump is running but no air bubbles are evident, then the

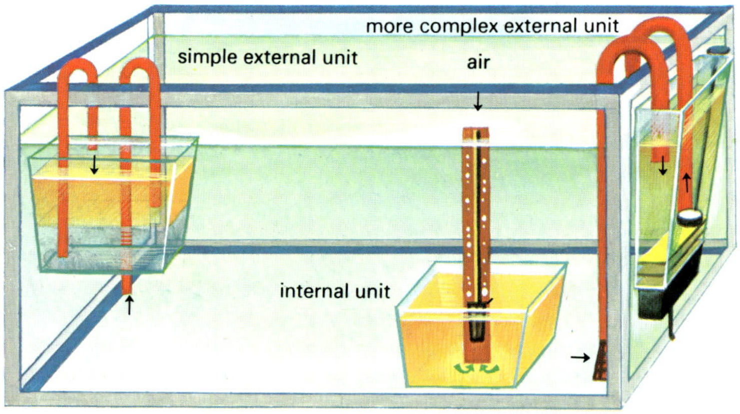

Filters should be fitted before the tank is filled or planted. External types are more easily-maintained than internal types which tend to get overlooked once the tank is fully planted

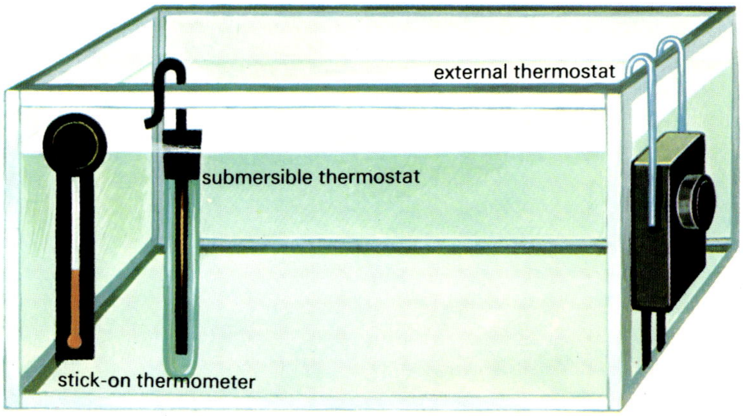

Although separate heaters can be used, with either internal or external thermostats, combined units are more popular.

Before furnishing the tank, make sure it is on a firm, level base. The final aquarium will be very heavy and cannot be moved once completed

Once the biological (sub-gravel) filter has been installed, the gravel and rocks will hide it and the other aquarium equipment from direct view

Fill the aquarium gently to avoid disturbing the gravel contours. Use a jar (or saucer) to disperse the water flow

The correct manner of planting leaves the junction between plant stem and root system just above the gravel

airvalves must be opened further; if, say, one airstone works but not the air-operated filter (or vice versa) the air-valves require adjustment to balance the airflow between the two pieces of equipment. The waterflow from under-gravel filters need not be too excessive, a steady flow is all that is required. Occasionally, an airlock inside the power filter body prevents water from reaching the impeller, gently rocking the filter body to and fro will dislodge the air and allow water to flow.

After a few hours the water temperature will have stabilized; take the reading on the thermometer, it should be around 25 °C. If it is too high, or too low, **SWITCH OFF THE POWER** and adjust the thermostat control by a slight amount in the required direction. Switch on the power again and allow some time to elapse before rechecking. Repeat this stage as required.

During the first few weeks after setting up, the biological filter will gradually become 'matured', that is, the bacterial colony will slowly develop. Adding some gravel from an established aquarium will hasten this procedure as will the introduction of a few hardy fishes. During this settling-in period, treat the aquarium as if it was fully stocked with the exception of adding food (unless a few fish are present). Under the influence of regular illumination the plants will start to develop their root systems and any that have floated up can be gently reset in the gravel.

Once the water clears and everything looks a little more established you can begin to think about introducing some of your chosen fishes.

Looking After *Your Fish*

No amount of technical equipment can replace proper care and understanding. In nature, fishes will swim away from danger or poor water conditions, seeking out a better environment. In the close confines of the aquarium, this is not possible and responsibility for the fishes health and welfare is all yours. The process of getting to know fish is very important; each species has its own characteristic behaviour and you must manage the population within your aquarium accordingly. An off-colour fish reveals itself by its appearance or behaviour and swift remedial action can be taken. The equipment is simple to operate, reliable and proven in its efficiency — the more important 'variables' to learn about concern the fish themselves and how to supply their basic needs.

It is a good idea to keep the lively Tiger Barb, Barbus tetrazona, *in shoals otherwise they may turn their individual attention towards nipping the fins of slower-moving fish in the tank*

CHOOSING HEALTHY STOCK

New fishes should be as healthy as can be ascertained at the time of purchase. Do not buy fish that look emaciated or that have obvious wounds, spots, blisters or any other outward sign of illness. (Split fins may be the result of mishandling during transit and, although they may eventually heal, the splits are an entry point for disease in an aquarium where water conditions are poor.) The fish should be able to swim without effort and to remain at any chosen location in the water without losing stability. Think twice about buying fish from any tank that contains a dead fish, even if the species you want may be different. On the other hand, fishes hiding away in a dealer's tank may not be doing so out of illness; they may be sharing a tank with unsuitable companions or may be nocturnal species.

A contributory cause of disease is stress. During its journey to your home from its original source (native jungle stream or commercial breeding station), the fish have had a traumatic journey with several changes of water conditions. Make the transfer from shop to home aquarium as stress-free as possible. Carry the fish home in a plastic bag in a dark container, ideally a heat-insulated case. Float the plastic bag in the aquarium for some 20 minutes to equalize the water temperatures, even running a little aquarium water into the bag to partially acclimatize the fish to your aquarium's water conditions. At the end of this period gently tilt the bag over and allow the fish to swim out.

To avoid introducing disease into the aquarium with new arrivals, quarantine them in a separate small tank for two to three weeks, during which time any latent disease should show itself. Conditions in the quarantine tank must be kept up to the same standard of cleanliness as those in the main tank.

Right: Carrying the fishes home in a heat-insulated box will prevent them becoming chilled during the journey

FEEDING

All animals require an input of 'fuel' to provide them with energy and 'building blocks' to develop and repair body tissues. Perhaps the greatest problem with feeding aquarium fishes is maintaining enough variety in their diet. The beginner may wonder how the equivalent of a wild fish's diet can be provided in captivity. Fortunately, much research has been carried out by the pet food manufacturers and their products are based on studies of fishes nutritional requirements.

Far right: Surface-feeding fishes can reach these worms much more easily through the use of this floating worm-feeder

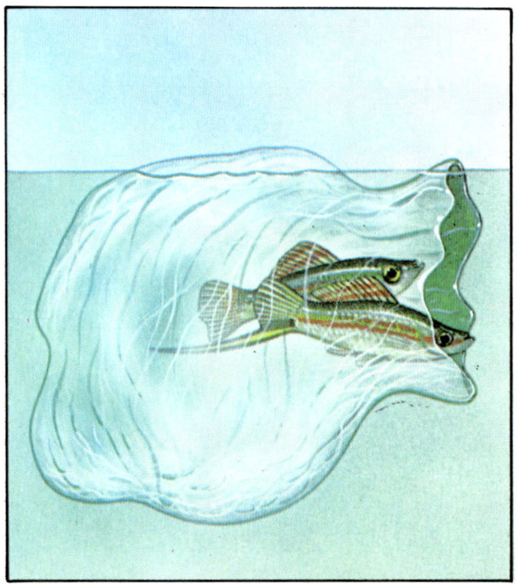

Right: After floating the fishes' bag in the aquarium for several minutes, to equalize the water temperatures, allow the fish to swim out into the aquarium of their own accord: tipping them out will stress them

Modern manufactured fish foods are excellent but a monotonous diet based just on one type should be avoided. Fish in the wild find different foods according to the time of year – in the tropical rainy season for instance flooding brings extra 'drowned' insects to the fish. Fruit from overhanging trees may also pro-

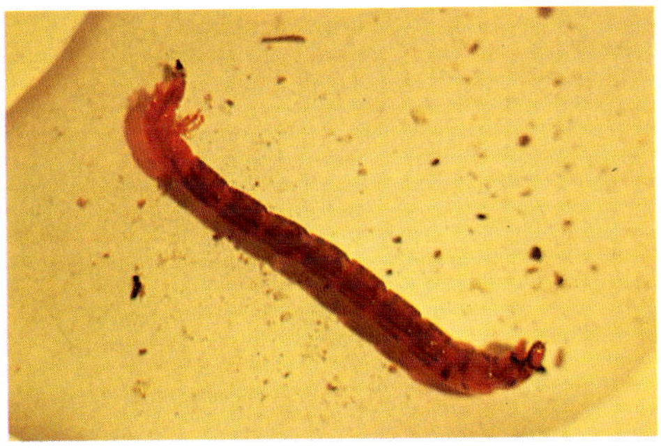

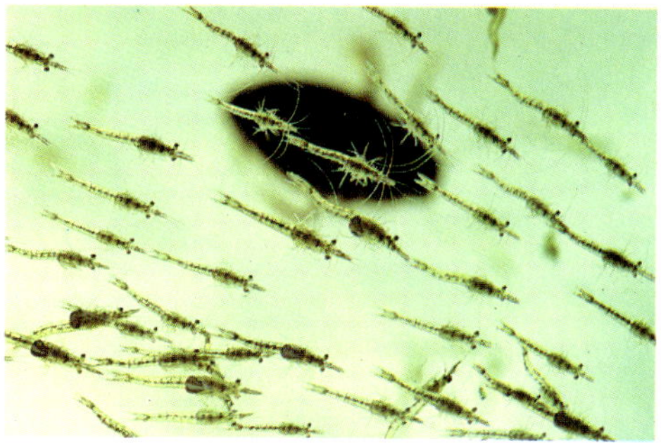

*Far left: Bloodworms, (*Chironomus larvae*) often found in rain butts make excellent live food for fishes*

Left: Buy live Mysis Shrimp from you dealer regularly as a frequent delicacy for your fishes

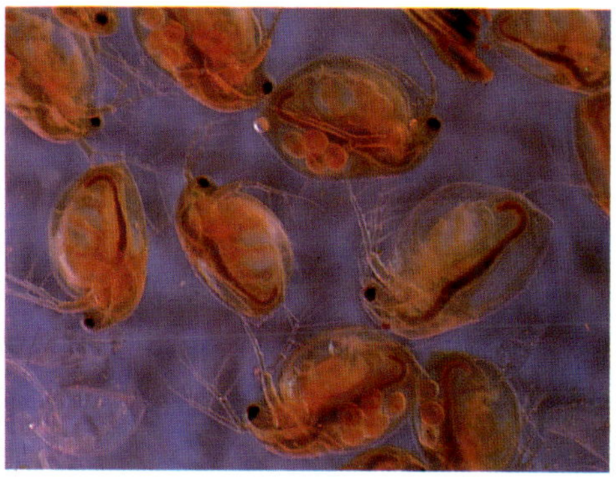

*Far left: Some dealers have developed this neat way to pre-package Glassworms (*Chaoborus larvae*)*

Left: The ever-popular Water Flea, Daphnia, *can be caught from standing waters such as ornamental ponds or purchased from dealers*

vide seasonal food. Then there is always the possibility of a tasty snack of waterborne animals and, of course, smaller fishes! Such natural foods cannot easily be replaced by artificial substitutes but by *varying* the types of good quality commercial foods you give your fish, you will be doing your best to keep them interested in their daily intake. Pay extra attention to those fishes with definite food requirements – vegetarian and carnivorous tendencies are well catered for by the fish-food manufactures.

Presentation of food is also very important. Unless the fish is given food in a form it can accept and in a manner it is expecting, it may not get its fair share or the food it does get will not be doing it the most good. It would be pointless, for example, giving a nocturnal, bottom-dwelling fish (such as many catfishes) floating flake foods with the tank lights still ablaze. Quick-sinking foods, given after the tank lights are switched off, are much more beneficial. The Golden Rule of feeding is **little and perhaps not too often**. Offer no more than will be consumed in a few minutes. Uneaten food remaining in the aquarium will cause water pollution.

Dried foods (flakes, tablets and granules of various mixtures of ingredients) can be supplemented with live foods. Live foods fall into two groups – aquatic and terrestrial.

Live foods

Aquatic foods are, of course, the most natural but their use does include some risk, particularly if the food is collected either from fish-inhabited or polluted waters. In either case, disease or predators may be carried into the aquarium along with the food and transmitted to your fishes. Before feeding, such foods should be thoroughly cleansed by being stored in running or constantly renewed water for some hours. Examples of good aquatic foods are the Water Flea (*Daphnia pulex*), *Cyclops*, *Tubifex* worms, and gnat, midge and mosquito larvae. The first two can be collected from ponds (ornamental ponds in public parks are good sources but do obtain permission first) reasonably easily; collection of *Tubifex* worms is best left to the experts for two reasons – it is a very specialized and messy job for a start and only the experts are likely to know the best, albeit rapidly diminishing, sites. Increasing efforts to reduce river pollution has made the supply of tubificid worms less dependable. Fish owners who have water butts in their gardens will find colonies of gnat, midge and mosquito larvae in the water during the summer. The larvae make excellent food and do much to bring fish into sparkling condition; also collect the pupal stage following larval life, it is just as nutritious.

Terrestrial live foods are based mainly on 'worms'. The humble earthworm is an excellent source of food: small worms will be taken whole by larger fishes but you will have to shred or chop up larger worms for smaller fishes. Do not collect worms from areas of the garden previously treated with fertilizer or pesticides for obvious reasons. Some red brandling-type worms from compost heaps are not suitable.

A much smaller worm, ideal as a starter food for young fishes, can be cultivated in cereal-based cultures. Whiteworms are about 2 cm ($\frac{3}{4}$ in) long and not much thicker than stout thread. They reproduce rapidly when kept on a moist earth/peat/loam mixture and fed with cereals. The related, but smaller, grindalworm is similarly cultured but may require a little more warmth for successful raising. Microworms are cultured in a thin cereal paste rather than over earth. In all these examples, future cultures of food can be assured by taking new cultures as the old comes to an end – your nose will tell you when it is time to do this.

The best cultured livefood for young fishes is undoubtedly the newly-hatched young of the Brine Shrimp (*Artemia salina*). Brine Shrimp eggs can be purchased from your aquatic dealer and can be hatched in a warm saltwater solution in around 24–26 hours. The tiny living food is very nutritious, and it is a good idea to start successive hatchings off at daily intervals so that your young fishes have a constant supply during their earliest growing stages. The great advantage these cultured foods have over wild-caught live foods is that they are absolutely disease-free.

Fish can be tempted with all manner of food: swatted, not pesticide-killed, houseflies may be taken, as may their larval forms. Crickets, grasshoppers and woodlice are also possibilities. Small chunks of lean meat can be hung in the aquarium for fish to peck at; tinned peas, bruised lettuce leaves, scalded spinach leaves, wheatgerm flakes etc, can all be offered, but fish have to be educated on to a new food, so offer a little at a time and remove it if uneaten. Starving the fish for a few days often makes them try a new food a little more willingly.

Holidays

Holidays should pose no problems for the fishkeeper. Provided the fish have been well fed, they can remain up to two weeks without food quite happily. If a neighbour is going to feed them, impress upon them the importance of only giving small portions once a day. A simple strategy is to prepare pre-packed daily feeds for your neighbour to use.

DISEASES

Early diagnosis of disease is imperative if treatment is to be successful. Learn to spot signs of abnormal behaviour, changes in appearance and coloration. Loss of appetite and sluggish or reluctant movement are all pointers to something wrong. A good time to look for signs of trouble is at feeding time when all the fish are gathered together and comparisons can be made quite easily. Fortunately, most of the diseases with external symptoms are easily recognized and cured. Internal disorders are usually diagnosed too late for an effective cure. Veterinary surgeons are becoming more aware of fish problems and will be happy to give advice in the more difficult areas of fish health and treatment; you will also need to seek a vet's help when obtaining modern antibiotic remedies.

The following diseases are some most commonly found in aquariums but, hopefully, with good aquarium management they should not bother your fishes too often.

Anchor worm (*Lernaea*)

Lernaea can be clearly seen clinging to the side of the fish, and the fish repeatedly rubs itself against rocks etc. in an effort to dislodge it. Although physical removal is one method of dealing with the parasite, a wound will be left which could become infected. Alternatively, remove the fish and touch the worm with a small brush dipped in potassium permanganate. This kills the parasite which usually falls off. A further method is to use a proprietary cure.

Fish louse

The scratching actions of the fish indicate the presence of an irritating parasite. The fish louse (*Argulus*) attaches itself to the host by suckers. Physical removal is possible, but with reservations as for *Lernaea*. Local application of a drop of strong salt solution may also be effective. *Argulus* and *Lernaea* may inadvertently be introduced with pond-caught live foods.

Flukes

Flukes may be one of two microscopic parasites infecting the fish's skin (*Gyrodactylus*) or the delicate gill membranes (*Dactylogyrus*).

Gyrodactylus causes the fish's colours to fade and the skin becomes slimy, sometimes with blood spots. *Dactylogyrus* affects the gill membranes and the fish will pant at the water surface with its gills inflamed and extended. Affected fishes should be isolated in a well-aerated treatment tank and given baths of proprietary remedies.

Fishes panting at the surface are not always affected by gill fluke; low oxygen levels in the water may be to blame – especially in overcrowded tanks in very warm weather – and the fish have been driven to the surface to gulp air. A rapid increase in aeration will bring relief, but thinning out the fish population into other tanks will also do a lot to help.

White Spot (*Ichthyophthirius*)

The best known fish disease; every aquarium is affected at one time or another. The symptoms are well-described by the common name – tiny white spots cover the body and fins.

This parasitic disease has a three-stage cyclic lifestyle – as visible spots on the victim, as a dormant cyst and a free-swimming period when it is searching for a fresh victim. It can only be successfully dealt with during the free-swimming time. The aquarium should be treated using one of the many very effective proprietary remedies. Some plants may be adversely affected.

Velvet disease (*Oodinium*)

The symptoms of this disease are similar to those of white spot but *Oodinium* covers the body with much smaller spots giving a velvety or gold dust effect from which the disease takes its name. The whole aquarium can be treated with commercially-available remedies.

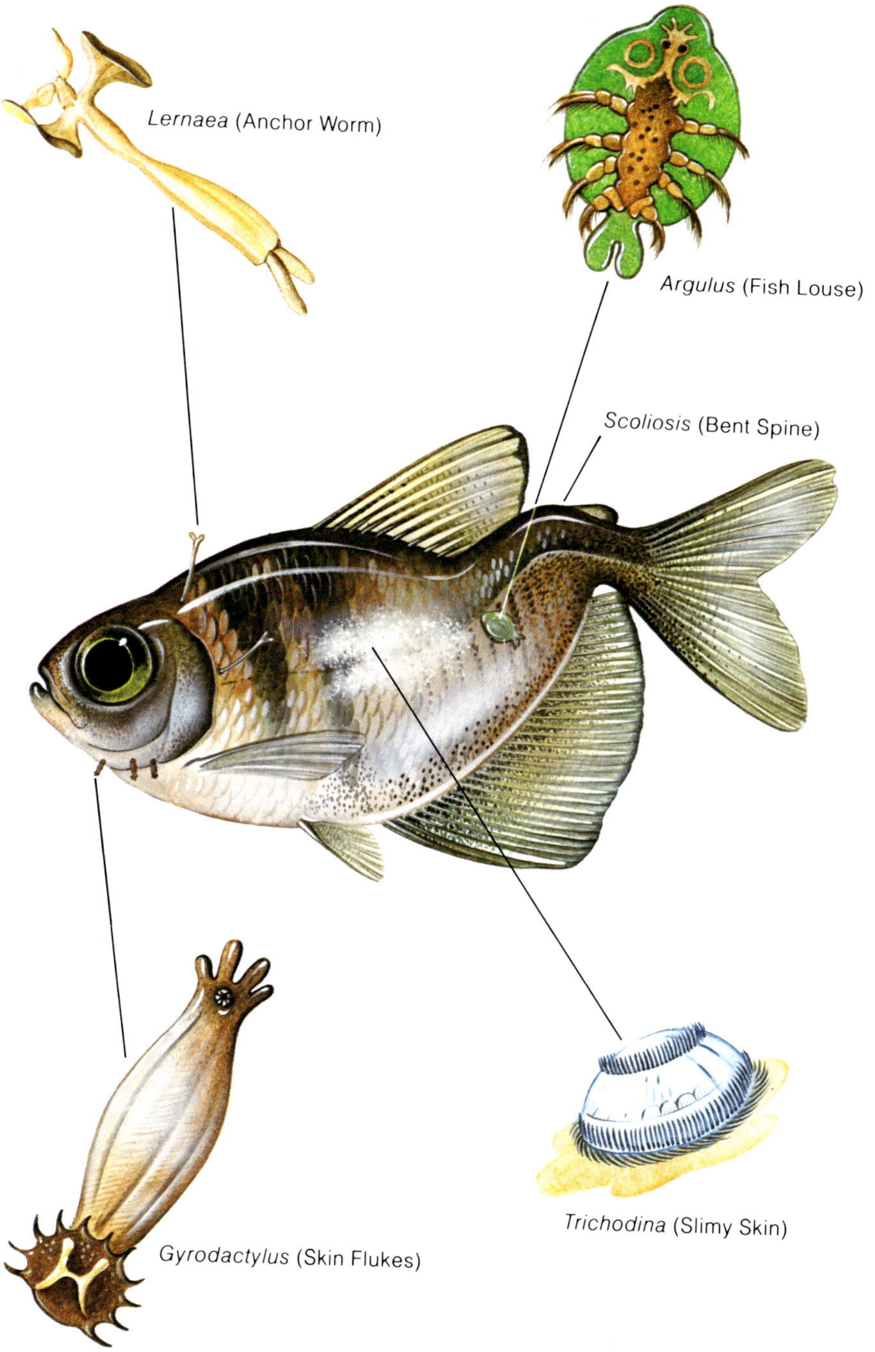

Above: Fish parasites. This illustration shows several parasites that attack fishes, although it is unlikely that all will strike at the same time

Left: This Cherry Barb, Barbus titteya, *is heavily infested with White Spot disease,* Ichthyophthirius, *but proprietary remedies are very safe and rapidly effective*

Fungus
Fungus is more common in coldwater fishes but tropical attacks are caused by the same microorganism, the water mould *Saprolegnia*. In all cases the fish is covered with a cotton-wool like growth.

Simple salt baths are effective but modern broad-spectrum remedies are far superior and easily administered. Treatment takes the form of a prolonged (weak strength) or short term (high concentration) bath.

'Mouth fungus'
Although this disease is not caused by a fungus, and does not respond to anti-fungus remedies, the fluffy white growth around the mouth has given rise to the common name. It is caused by a slime bacterium which is unaffected by regular fungus remedies. Proprietary treatments are available commercially or antibiotics may be obtained from a qualified veterinary surgeon.

Right: When an eye protrudes to this extent it is known as Exophthalmus *and is due to a build-up of fluid immediately behind the eye*

Far right: This Red Wagtail Platy is suffering from Fin Rot; the rays of the caudal fin are decaying away. It is important not to allow the damage to reach the body of the fish. Proprietary remedies are effective but the aquarium conditions must also be checked and remedied too

Finrot
Fins damaged by careless handling or as a result of fighting with other fish will be affected by finrot if aquarium conditions are not up to standard. The tissue between the fin rays gradually disintegrates. Surgical removal of the affected part and improving aquarium conditions will help as the fin usually regrows in time. Proprietary remedies are also helpful but the best prevention is to keep conditions up to scratch.

Eye diseases
Eyes are sometimes affected by eye fungus or become cloudy. They may even protrude from the socket. Some proprietary remedies are said to be effective but as most eye infections are brought about by poor water conditions, the remedy (or rather the prevention) is obvious.

Dropsy
The symptoms are obvious, the body of the fish swelling up so that the scales stand out. Dropsy is contagious and the victim should be removed immediately. The cause of this disease is unknown and treatment is not always successful. Antibiotics can be effective, whilst drainage of the accumulated fluid in the body needs skilful work with a hypodermic needle and a sure hand.

Tuberculosis
Fish affected by tuberculosis are colourless and listless. They appear to feed normally but gradually fade away until they are totally emaciated. Confirmation of the disease is usually only possible at post mortem. Sporadic successes with antibiotic treatments have been reported but the diagnosis and treatment of tuberculosis is beyond a newcomer to the hobby.

Swimming disorders
Such disorders may be caused by disease or damage to the swim bladder itself, or be the result of diseases in neighbouring organs which cause it to malfunction.

If the swim bladder becomes affected, the fish's equilibrium will be affected and it will either tumble over and over or be unable to maintain a stationary position. Such disorders may be contributed to by chilling or deficiencies in the diet.

'Shimmying'

This is not a disease in itself, but a symptom of chilling or a reaction to new water conditions. Fish undulating from side to side without any forward motion are displaying typical symptoms of chilling. A rise in water temperature generally effects a successful recovery.

Treatment of affected fishes

Large visible parasites on individual fishes are best treated as single cases, fish being removed for treatment separately. A contagious disease such as White Spot is better dealt with by treating the whole aquarium.

If you follow the habit of quarantining any new fish, the quarantine tank can be used as a treatment tank. It only needs heating equipment, aeration and simple filtration facilities. Many remedies reduce the amount of oxygen in the water and extra aeration should be supplied. Biological and carbon-filled filters should not be used; the bacterial colonies may be adversely affected by the medication used (especially copper-based ones) and the carbon will remove the medication from the water by adsorption. Use a dimmer lamp (or shield the tank if fluorescent tubes are used) as many remedies will also be neutralized by bright light. A few plastic plants will give the fish a sense of security; real plants will not thrive under the dim lighting and may be adversely affected by the medication. When transferring fish to and from the treatment tank, do not risk spreading disease by using the same net in other tanks; sterilize nets after use with boiling water and a mild disinfectant.

When treating an established aquarium dosage may be difficult to calculate due to rocks and decorations displacing an unknown quantity of water. Treating fish in a separate bare tank makes for more accurate dosage.

Following successful treatment, water in the hospital tank should be gradually replaced with fresh to acclimatize the fish to its original water conditions before returning to the main aquarium.

Left: *The very tiny spots covering the sides and fins of this Indian Glassfish are the symptoms of Oodinium,* Velvet Disease

Fish with skin parasites often swim erratically

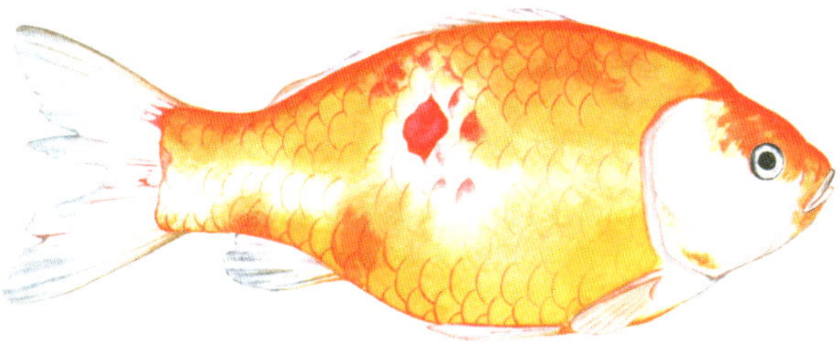

This Goldfish has 'Hole in the Body' Disease

Breeding

Why breed aquarium fishes? The reasons are several. It allows you to increase your fish stocks with minimum outlay, and successful breeding can be taken as sure confirmation that you are keeping your fish under almost ideal conditions. The thrill of watching your fish produce young is fascinating in its own right, especially as you see the more advanced species tending their offspring with as much concentration as any human. A more serious aspect concerns conservation. The hobbyist can, by breeding fishes in captivity, ensure that domestic supplies are continued, thus eliminating the need for continuous collection from the wild of endangered or otherwise 'hard-to-come-by' species. Finally, most people love a challenge and this area of fishkeeping has more than its fair share, especially in breeding fishes that have a reputation for being difficult, or new species about whose reproductive methods little is known. Professional ichthyologists may be more involved with the classification of species, not always concerning themselves with actual breeding, and this is an area where the hobbyist can contribute to scientific knowledge.

Ideally suited for the community aquarium, the Sheepshead Acara, Aequidens curviceps, *provides a perfect example of parental care in cichlids*

Livebearing male fishes have their anal fins adapted for reproductive purposes: that of the Swordtail (A) is fully modified and can be moved in any direction (bottom sequence: right – at rest, left – in fertilizing position). Those of the Goodeid and Halfbeak males (B, C) are only partly modified and not flexible at all

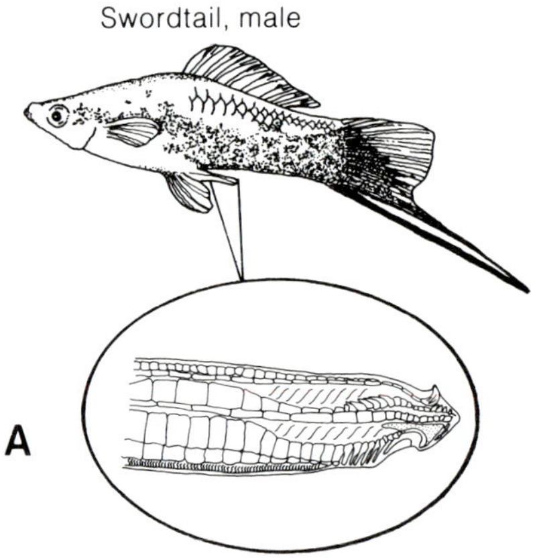

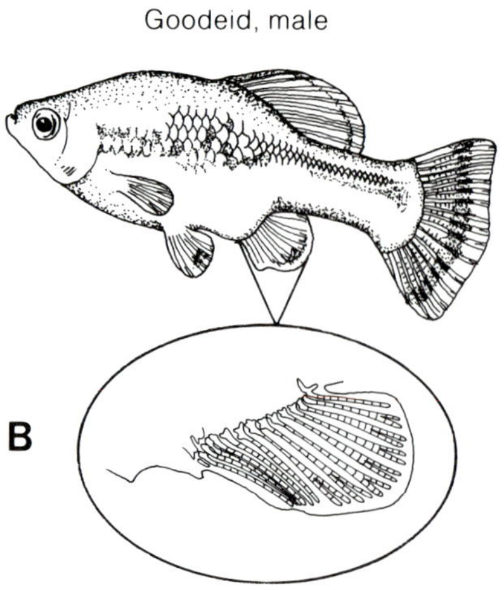

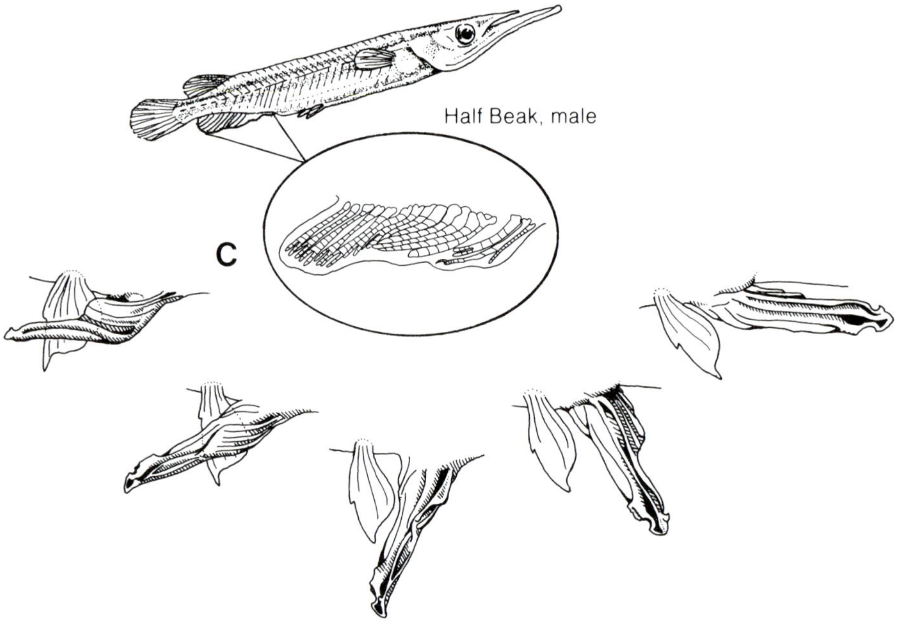

METHODS OF REPRODUCTION

There are several methods of reproduction, ranging from the haphazard to the highly sophisticated.

The majority of fish reproduce by producing eggs which are externally fertilized. This basic strategy has been refined in various groups of fishes. At its most basic, eggs are scattered by the females and fertilized haphazardly by males, the eggs drifting away on water currents to take their own chances on successful survival. The next development is the production of sticky eggs which become trapped in water plants that offer them some protection. Fish from waters that seasonally dry up completely lay their fertilized eggs in the streambed mud where they survive, hatching being triggered off by the stream refilling at the onset of the rainy season. Parental care of eggs and subsequent young is practised by fishes such as the Cichlids, Anabantids and some catfishes. Cichlids usually select and pre-clean a spawning site on which their eggs are laid, fertilized and guarded until hatching occurs; spawning sites may be out in the open or inside caves. Other Cichlids practise mouthbrooding, where the female not only incubates the fertilized eggs in her mouth but also allows the young free-swimming fry the sanctuary of her mouth again when danger threatens. Gouramies and some catfishes build bubble-nests out of saliva and maybe pieces of plants in which fertilized eggs are placed to hatch. The prize for the most original breeding method must go to the Splashing Tetra which lays and fertilizes its eggs *out of water* in order to protect them from predators.

In livebearing fishes the eggs are fertilized and hatch within the female's body. Miniature free-swimming fishes emerge from the mother ready to fend for themselves. Some female livebearers can store sperm in their body, so producing successive broods of young without re-mating.

SELECTING BREEDING STOCK

Successful breeding needs a true pair of fishes in the prime of life. Choosing a pair of fishes is harder than you might think, for many species keep the secret of sex differentiation pretty well hidden.

Far left: *The male* Aulonocara *displays egg-spots in the anal fin*

Left: *The female mouthbrooder,* Astatotilapia burtoni, *picks up fertilized eggs to incubate them orally*

Far left: *By pecking at the male's egg-spots, the female* A. burtoni *stimulates the release of sperm*

Left: *Female with young fry. Despite being free-swimming the fry will still seek refuge in the mother's mouth if danger threatens*

Livebearing fishes are a little more accommodating in this respect, as there is a clear difference between the anal fins of males and females. In egglaying species, male fishes have generally more colour, longer fins and are slimmer than females. The female owes her regular plumpness to the development of eggs within her body. Many fishes will spawn collectively, so putting all the slim fishes in with all the plump ones and letting them get on with it usually overcomes sex-selection difficulties.

To produce strong, best quality offspring the parent fishes must be in good condition themselves. Some fishes prefer to select their own mates, forming a strong bond, but where it is possible to select parents for their own inherent characteristics, then choose vigorous, well-coloured fishes with well-formed fins and no physical deformities or other defects. Depending on the method of spawning, it is usually a good idea to separate the sexes from each other two or three weeks before you put them together to spawn. Give them high quality foods, with a predominance of live foods if possible.

Above: *Some fishes change colour at breeding time:* Neetroplus nematopus

Above: *When spawning the male* Neetroplus nematopus *changes to this much darker pattern, almost a complete reversal of colours*

SPAWNING

With egglaying species, put the female into the breeding tank ahead of the male, say in the evening, and then introduce the male next morning. You should stay around in order to rescue the female should the male attack her if he considers she is not ready to spawn. The breeding tank should be planted quite thickly to provide shelter for the female. After spawning takes place, which can be a very active process, remove the female, and the male too if he is not required to tend the eggs. Again, this will depend on the species concerned. It may also be necessary to add some bactericide to the water to prevent the fertilized eggs from 'fungussing'; in some cases, shading the tank will be advantageous as some eggs are light sensitive (using bactericide will colour the water, thus shielding the eggs from light in the process.)

In most cases the eggs hatch after a day or two (you may need a magnifying glass to spot the tiny fish clinging to the plants or the front glass). The activity of

Below: The breeding tank should be furnished to suit the particular spawning actions of the fishes to be bred

Dense bushy plants will trap the eggs of Characins

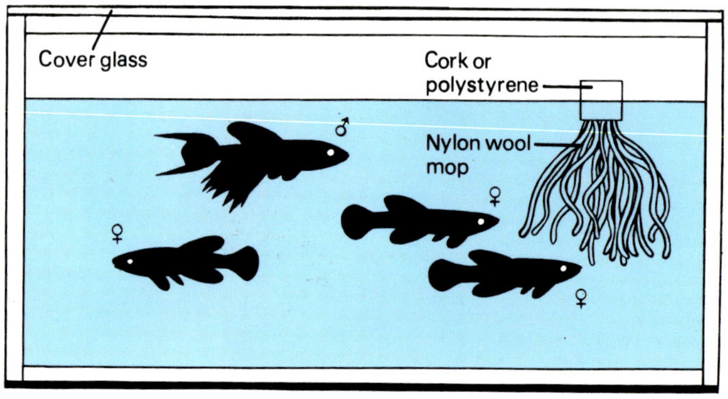

The floating artificial nylon mop allows easy collection of Killifish eggs

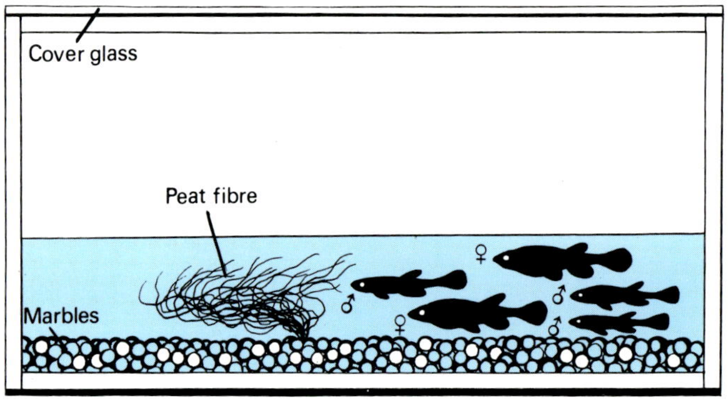

Shallow water, peat fibre and a layer of marbles cut down the risk of egg-eating by Barbs and Danios

Some Killifishes dive into a deep layer of peat in which to fertilize and lay their eggs

The Cichlid breeding aquarium needs flat rocks, caves (or flower pots) depending on the species to be bred.

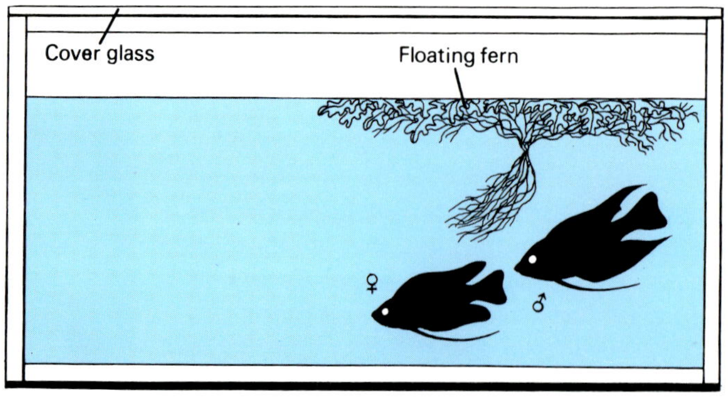

Bubblenesting fishes appreciate some floating plants in which to construct their nests

the parents in the case of species that practise parental care will show you how things are progressing.

Livebearing fishes require a slightly different technique. The actual mating is a fleeting affair. The female then becomes *gravid* (pregnant) and delivers her young in about four weeks. She should be given a separate small well-planted tank to herself, being transferred to it well in advance of her expected delivery date, otherwise she will give birth prematurely to immature young. After birth takes place, the young will have the safety of the plants to hide in, and the mother can be given a few days rest in the same tank to recover before being put back into the main collection again.

Obviously, the fact that livebearers give birth so readily (and predictably) means that they are ideal material for 'line-breeding' and the development of new colour strains. You must be very watchful that no inadvertent 'crossing' occurs that could spoil the strain, and most livebearer-fanciers limit their efforts to a single strain to reduce this possibility.

RAISING THE YOUNG FISH

With young fish (*fry*) from egglaying species, you must provide the tiniest of food for them (see page 30) gradually increasing the size and amount as they mature. Partial water changes will help to keep the tank water clean, as the use of powerful filtration systems will not be practicable.

Livebearer fry are able to take slightly larger food (crushed flake food) than egglayer young right from birth. Both sets of young will develop quickly on a steady diet of newly-hatched brine shrimp, microworm, grindalworm, shredded *Tubifex*, and screened *Daphnia*. Do not attempt to raise the entire batch of young. Mortalities are bound to occur, and you should also discard any malformed specimens; the aim should be to raise quality not quantity.

Left, top: *Brine Shrimp may be easily hatched in aerated salt warm water; turning off the air and blowing down the short tube will empty newly-hatched shrimp into a net where they may be rinsed before feeding to young fish*

Left, below: *Jars of* Infusoria *can be stood above the aquarium and the food slowly siphoned into the tank through a clamped tube. Alternatively, regular feedings can be made by means of an eye-dropper*

Fish
Anatomy

Getting to know your fishes is one of the most enjoyable parts of fishkeeping. This is done mainly by straightforward recognition of the fish's overall 'design' – primarily its shape and colour patterns. To understand the fish further you will need a more detailed familiarization – with its anatomy: for instance, sexing the fishes requires a close observation of the external features; again, when diagnosing diseases, knowledge of where and what to look for will be all the more easy if the general anatomical details are second-nature to you. In the catalogue of fish species, too (see page 47), reference will be made to several physical features of fish. To familiarize the reader with them, this short introduction to fish anatomy has been prepared.

Even though the physical characteristics of this Painted Catfish, Pimelodella picta, *have evolved away from the normal, such changes have occurred to suit the fish's lifestyle more exactly*

BODY SHAPES

Although a fish's shape is so familiar, there are variations on the expected symmetrical silhouette that may need explanation. Body shapes have evolved, or become adapted, to suit the fish's particular life style.

A body with a flat or straight top (dorsal) surface allows the fish to swim immediately below the surface without the body breaking water. Eyes set high on this body, coupled with an upturned mouth make finding and taking food from the surface very easy.

A body that is symmetrically contoured top and bottom usually has a mouth situated at the tip of the snout on a line horizontal with the centre of the body. Such fishes inhabit the midwater levels taking food from any level without difficulty.

A flat-bottomed body profile makes an inefficient aerofoil section, but it is just because of this that it is useful to bottom-dwelling fishes in fast-flowing waters – they cannot be lifted off the streambed by water currents. The flattened shape brings their downturned mouths that much nearer to the streambed where their food is to be found.

Torpedo-shaped fishes usually have deeply-forked tails (caudal fins) and can travel very fast through the water. Disk-shaped bodies are a feature of more slowly-moving fishes or of fishes frequenting more sluggish water courses. A body that is compressed laterally enables fishes such as the Angelfish and Discus to slip easily between the stems of reedbeds.

Mouth positions have evolved to suit the fish's eating habits (see page 9); even the structure of the mouth can change to assist in this matter. The Leaf-fish, for example, has a protrusible trumpetlike mouth which is extended as its prey passes, the inrush of water into the mouth carrying the prey in with it. Alga-eating fishes (some African Cichlids and the Sucking Catfishes) have rasping bristles on the lips to help tear algae from the rock surface (and are useful in keeping an aquarium clean).

Although a catfish, the body shape of Dianema urostriata *is adapted better for midwater swimming*

The Discus, Symphysodon *spp, has a tall laterally-compressed body which allows it to glide effortlessly between the river bank reed-stems; its vertical bars also provide camouflage*

FINS

The majority of fishes have seven fins: three single fins and two sets of paired fins. The dorsal fin is carried vertically on top of the fish's back; this fin, along with a corresponding downward mounted fin on the ventral (under) surface of the fish, the anal fin, helps to stabilize the fish against any sideways rolling movement in the same manner as a ship's keel. Rainbowfishes have two separate dorsal fins. In male livebearing fishes the anal fin has become adapted into a reproductive organ, the gonopodium. The fish's main forward propulsive force comes from a combination of a waving motion of the body terminating in sideways sweeps of the caudal fin, better known as the tail. On each side of the body, just behind the gill cover emerge the pectoral fins; almost immediately beneath them emerging from the bottom of the fish (but ahead of the anal fin) are the two ventral or pelvic fins. The pectoral and ventral fins correspond to mammals' limbs and give the fish both manoeuvrability and braking controls. Some fishes (Gouramies) have taste buds located in the tips of their ventral fins, some female catfishes use theirs to carry eggs, whilst Angelfish use their pectoral fins to constantly fan their fertilized eggs so that dirt does not settle on them while hatching occurs.

Characins and some catfishes have an extra fin, the adipose located on the back between the dorsal fin and the caudal. This is made of fatty tissues and its purpose is not known.

SCALES

Scales provide protection for the fish's skin and also streamline the fish. This, together with the mucus covering them, enables the fish to slip through the water more easily. Not all fishes have scales: the Armoured Catfish group (including *Corydoras* catfishes) have their body covered with two rows of overlapping bony plates known as scutes.

On the other hand, African catfishes have neither scales nor scutes and their skin is quite exposed.

BREATHING ORGANS

The fish extracts dissolved oxygen from the water by taking in water through its mouth and expelling it through its gill covers. As the water passes over the gills the oxygen diffuses out of the water into the tiny blood-filled gill membranes. There are one or two supplementary breathing methods to assist the fish when the oxygen content becomes very low. The Labyrinth group of fishes (*Betta splendens*, *Colisa*, *Trichogaster* etc.) are so known because they have a convoluted, labyrinth-like auxiliary organ sited in the head near the gills. Here, moist atmospheric air is stored and the oxygen extracted. *Corydoras* catfish are often seen dashing up to the water surface and taking in a gulp of air. This air is passed into the hind gut where, again, oxygen is extracted.

TEETH

The best-known instance of fish teeth is found in the Piranha fish, a member of the Characin group; even its small relative the Neon Tetra has similar teeth, as do all Characins. Fishes such as Barbs, Danios and Rasboras also have teeth but not in the mouth. Their teeth are situated in the throat and are known as pharyngeal teeth and are used to grind up food against a hard bony pad.

SWIM BLADDER

Fishes have an internal swim bladder that acts as a hydrostatic organ, providing the fish with neutral density and allowing it to remain at any chosen level in the water without exerting a conscious effort to do so.

LATERAL LINE SYSTEM

If you examine the flanks of a fish you will see a horizontal row of scales, usually running the whole length of the fish, with a tiny hole in the centre of each scale. The effect is as if a dotted line has been drawn along the side of the fish. Vibrations in the surrounding water are picked up by a sensitive nervous system linked to these tiny holes, and the fish is able to detect obstacles in its path or the proximity of other fishes in muddy waters or in the dark.

Some fish (e.g. Elephant-noses, Knife-fish) have a more sophisticated detection and navigation system. They generate a weak electromagnetic field around themselves and by detecting alterations in the strength of this field (caused by nearby objects or other fishes) can 'see' their way around the tank without necessarily using their eyes. Again, a very useful aid in dark or muddy waters.

COLOUR

Colour can be due to two separate biochemical processes. A crystalline waste product from the kidneys known as guanin is not excreted from the body but stored beneath the skin. Depending on the position of the crystals, various reflected colours are seen. Notice how the colours, or sheen, of the fish changes when seen under side-lighting (say sunlight hitting the fish through the front glass) instead of light from the lamps in the reflector.

Colour can also be due to pigment in the skin cells. Dark colours are due to melanophores and some fish are able to contract or expand the colour cells at will giving a lighter or dark effect to the skin. This effect can be easily noticed when a silver fish with black stripes (Angelfish for instance) is excited or frightened and you can see the stripes fading or becoming more intense. Another example of wilful colour changes can be seen in

The electric-blue line of the Cardinal Tetra, Paracheirodon innesi, *is due to a layer of light-reflecting crystals of guanin deposited beneath the skin*

The African Killifish, Aphyosemion bivitattum, *uses its striking colour pattern as camouflage as it moves around its stream keeping to the shaded areas*

Pencilfishes which take on a distinctly different colour pattern at night.

Colour plays an important part in camouflaging the fish for protective purposes. The Angelfish's stripes hide it amongst reeds as do the lines on *Anostomus anostomus* which further assists the deception by resting head downwards. *Loricaria* catfishes and the Nandid *Badis badis* can both change their coloration to blend with their surroundings. Whereas most fish have a dark top surface, *Synodontis nigriventris* has a dark belly which similarly camouflages it when it swims upside down.

Below: The external features common to any fish may vary according to each fish's adaptation to its various physical needs

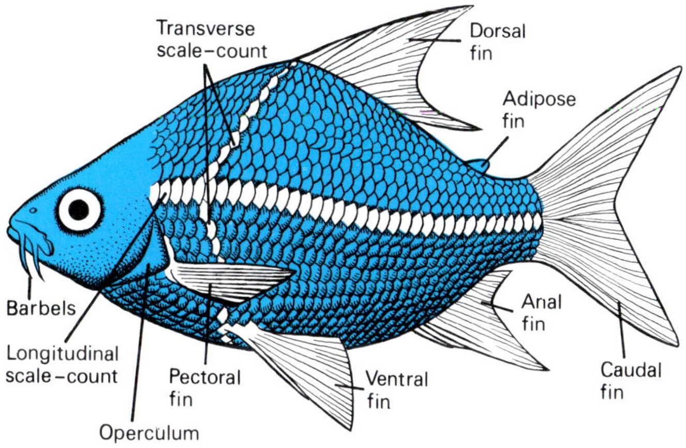

Fish
Descriptions

The following pages contain a wide selection of fishes, the majority of which are commonly available. One or two species have been included for their curiosity interest – these may be a little harder to find in the usual aquatic shops and a little 'shopping around' may be necessary if you want to try these fishes in your aquarium.

The fishes are arranged in alphabetical species order within popular hobbyist-recognized groups: to the purist, these groups may not be entirely scientifically accurate but to list species taxonomically in such a limited space would result in a very fragmented work.

Although most species have been chosen for their proven compatibility with each other, be guided by the notes given so that the correct aquarium conditions are provided to suit your own selection. Remember that the majority of fishes on display in the shops are juveniles so take note of the likely fully-mature aquarium sizes attained by fishes and avoid putting subsequent 'extremes-of-size' species together in the close confines of your aquarium.

Where a single fish is illustrated, a male is to be assumed unless stated otherwise; where two fishes are shown, the sex of each is indicated wherever possible. Sizes given are based on the mature size reached under aquarium conditions and are measured from tip of the snout to rear end of the body (the caudal fin is excluded). Where two sizes are given, the first relates to the male fish, the second to the female. This discrepancy of size between sexes is found most markedly in livebearing species.

The popular Angelfish, Pterophyllum scalare, *has many aquarium-developed varieties, including this extra long-finned form*

ANABANTIDS

Although the group of Climbing Perches, Fighting Fishes and Gouramies are commonly (albeit inaccurately) classed as Anabantids, technically they belong to several separate Families. These fishes are notable for possessing an auxiliary breathing organ known as the 'labyrinth' which allows them to make use of atmospheric air if necessary. Another special feature of one group, the Gouramies, is the adaptation of the ventral fins: these are highly-movable, and the fishes are often seen reaching forward with these fins (which have taste buds on their tips) to explore their surroundings for food.

Most are peaceful, the main exception being the Siamese Fighting Fish (*Betta splendens*) although males of other species are quite likely to become pugnacious towards any fish in the aquarium at breeding time.

These fishes are bubblenest-builders, the male building a floating nest of saliva bubbles and pieces of aquarium plants under which he entices the female to join him in a close embrace during which eggs are released and fertilized; the male usually guards the nest whilst the young hatch. It is vital that the spawning of these fishes is supervised, for if the female is not accepted by the male he will attack her violently. A well-planted breeding tank will give her opportunities to escape from him if necessary. The fry are very small and require food that is very small; green water and hard-boiled egg yolk, a suspension formed by squeezing through a cloth in water are practical solutions.

The Siamese Fighting Fish is a typical example of how the aquarium fish has been 'cultivated'. It has much more colour and far longer fins than the wild male. There are strict standards recognized by Fish Societies as regards the exhibiting of this fish.

The cultivated aquarium form of the Siamese Fighting Fish, Betta splendens, *bears little resemblance to the wild fish. Males will quarrel if kept together; females do not have the long well-developed fins*

Individual Species

Siamese Fighting Fish
Betta splendens
60 mm (2.5 in)
Thailand

In its native Thailand, the Siamese Fighting Fish is kept more for its pugnacity than for its good looks, the wild male *B. splendens* bearing little resemblance to the long-finned aquarium beauty. Maintained to fight for wagers, the Siamese Fighting Fish loses little of this natural talent in the more peaceful home aquarium, two males soon effecting a breach of the peace if kept in the same tank.

As a result of selective breeding, there are many cultivated colour forms and all serious fishkeepers conform to the rigid standards laid down for these fish when exhibited. According to some ideals, colours should be singular and extend fully into the fins, although some organizations may have slightly different standards to embrace fishes with other colour patterns. A popular variant on the normal single-coloured fish is the 'Cambodia Fighting Fish' where the body is cream-coloured with coloured fins.

The male has the best finnage; those of the female are much shorter and her coloration is very drab. Spawning follows the normal bubblenest-building pattern: the male creates a nest out of saliva bubbles perhaps amongst floating plants and then coaxes the female beneath it. A thickly-planted aquarium should be used for breeding so that the female can find refuge from the male if necessary, particularly if he rejects her as a breeding partner.

Honey Gourami
Colisa chuna
45 mm (2 in)
India

The golden-brown oblong body of the male is topped off by a vivid yellow dorsal fin and in spawning condition the throat region and forepart of the anal fin becomes turquoise. The long ventral fins are almost limited to a single ray but, like those of many other species in this group, are extremely mobile and equipped with taste cells. Will spawn readily in the usual bubblenest manner, at which time the male's pugnacity towards other fishes appears to be in strict inverse proportion to his physical size. The fry are very small and require the tiniest of first foods. The taxonomic name of this fish may be changed (subject to recent scrutiny) to *C. sota*.

Dwarf Gourami
Colisa lalia
60 mm (2.5 in)
Northeastern India

The vivid silvery-blue body is crossed diagonally with brilliant red stripes. The major fins are edged in red, the long delicate ventrals being red/orange. These beautiful colours become even more intense at spawning periods. The male is clearly the dominant partner and is very pugnacious indeed to other fishes (and to his prospective partner if he does not agree with your choice). The fry may be difficult to raise as they are very small, and mortality may be high during their early weeks: especially tiny foods are required. The related *C. fasciata* (Giant, Banded or Striped Gourami) is larger and similarly marked, but not so brilliantly coloured.

Spotted Climbing Perch
Ctenopoma acutirostre
150 mm (6 in)
Africa

A very attractive fish with dark spots on a golden background. Little is known about sexual differences but it has been surmised that the female has fewer spots. This species has a large mouth that can be extended to engulf any passing small fish, so it is best kept only with similar-sized fishes. The genus *Ctenopoma* contains either bubble-nesting species that care for their young or those that produce floating eggs which are not cared for at all by the parents. *C. acutirostre* belongs to the latter group.

Above: The African Spotted Climbing Perch, Ctenopoma acutirostre, *is far more predatory than the more decorative Asian-related species*

Left: The Honey Gourami, Colisa chuna, *is the smallest member of the* Colisa *genus*

Below: The popular Dwarf Gourami, Colisa lalia, *will breed readily but turns very aggressive towards any other fishes in the tank when doing so*

Giant Goramy
Osphronemus goramy
600 mm (24 in)
Great Sunda Islands

The fact that this fish is collected for food is not surprising when you consider its size! It requires a very large tank if it is to reach anywhere near its natural mature size and, of course plenty of food (especially vegetable materials). It builds a bubblenest with plants but aquarium spawnings have not been reported.

Above: The Giant Goramy is only suitable for the largest public aquariums

Lace, Leeri, Mosaic or Pearl Gourami
Trichogaster leeri
110 mm (4.5 in)
Far East

This fish has attracted several common names, a tribute to the differing opinions of those who have tried to capture its beauty in words. The lace or mosaic pattern of the body is crossed by a dark horizontal line running from snout to caudal fin. Males can be distinguished by the long trailing dorsal fin which reaches over the caudal fin. In spawning colours the male's ventral fins and front part of the anal fin become bright orange. This bubblenest builder often delays spawning until almost full-size is reached.

Moonlight Gourami
Trichogaster microlepis
150 mm (6 in)
Thailand

The clue is in the name: 'microlepis' means tiny-scaled, and you have to look hard to see the tiny scales that give the fish a burnished silver appearance. The slightly tipped up snout is typical. Like most fishes in the group, males have the longer and often more pointed fins.

The smooth silvery skin of the Moonlight Gourami, Trichogaster microlepis, *has very tiny scales for such a relatively-large fish*

Left: The male Leeri Gourami, Trichogaster leeri, *can be distinguished by the long dorsal fin and the trailing filaments to the anal fin*

Three-spot Gourami
Trichogaster trichopterus
110 mm (4.5 in)
Far East

The 'spots' include the eye which makes up the third together with two spots on the body. The basic light and dark blue body coloration can be variable, with dark wavy lines often seen. It is a more thicker-bodied fish than others in the genus. There are several colour variants of this fish ranging from blue to gold; some authorities have suggested that the latter may be a subspecies, *T. trichopterus sumatranus.*

Right: The Three-Spot Gourami, Trichogaster trichopterus, *is a well-established aquarium favourite and there are several colour variants*

The Sparkling Gourami, Trichopsis pumilus, *has beautiful blue eyes to set off against the dark red coloration*

Sparkling Gourami
Trichopsis pumilus
40 mm (1.5 in)
Far East

There are two surprising things about this fish – first its brilliant blue eyes, and secondly the croaking sound it occasionally makes, usually during spawning. The fins are sparkling blue (especially under side-lighting) with red edgings. The male may be distinguished by its slightly more pointed fins and a dark red edge right at the base of the anal fin. The bubblenest may be built under a broad-leaved plant and, not unexpectedly for a small fish, brood numbers are equally small, around 50 being quite normal.

CHARACINS

The species in this group number around 1300 of which over three-quarters are found in the New World. The most popular group within the family are the Tetras, relatively small colourful shoaling fishes. Being normally active during daylight, they are ideally suited for the well-lit aquarium. Almost all Characins (and their close relatives) have an adipose fin, and teeth in the jaws, the most notable example being the Piranha.

Dietary needs are usually easily satisfied. Most Characins are omnivorous, some are carnivorous and a few herbivorous. Larger Characins are predatory, especially those found in African lakes where many are caught for human consumption.

Characins are egg-scatterers; in the natural state the fish are not quite as interested in their fertilized eggs as Cyprinids but in the close confines of the aquarium it may be a different matter. Before spawning is attempted it is usual to separate the sexes for a week or two and feed them well; 'absence making the heart grow fonder' often ensures a willing pair of fishes which will provide you with good results.

Tetras

Bloodfin
Aphyocharax anisitsi
60 mm (2.5 in)
Argentina

Aptly-named, the fins are blood-red, but the apparently silver body will reveal a bluish sheen when the light catches it from the side. The male's anal fin has many tiny hooks (a spawning aid) which can become caught up in the net when handling the fish. A very active fish which looks best when kept as a fairly large shoal in a spacious aquarium. Spawning is easily accomplished, but again a large aquarium is required to accommodate the energetic driving of the female. Can be spawned collectively and precautions must be taken to save the eggs from the parent fish who will eat them given half a chance. Formerly *A. rubripinnis.*

Blind Cave Fish
Astyanax fasciatus mexicanus
95 mm (3.75 in)
Mexico

The main attraction of this basically pink, large Tetra-shaped fish is that the eyes have not developed. This is because the fish normally inhabits underground caves where light does not penetrate, thus making the possession of sight irrelevant; it has been reported that young fish often have functioning eyes which degenerate with increasing age. The fish finds its way around the aquarium quite effortlessly, using its sensitive lateral line system to warn it of obstacles, other fishes and even food in its path. Can be bred in the aquarium. Formerly known as *Anoptichthys jordani.*

The only area of strong colour on this species, Aphyocharax anisitsi, *is provided by the blood-red fins which also give the fish its popular name*

Left: *The main attraction of the Blind Cave Fish,* Astyanax fasciatus mexicanus, *for the aquarium is to show hobbyists just how well it can cope, unaffected by its natural lack of sight. It navigates around even the most crowded tank by means of its lateral line nervous system, not needing its eyes at all*

The Black Widow, Gymnocorymbus ternetzi, *is a very attractive fish when young, but it loses most of the sooty-black appearance with age*

Black Widow
Gymnocorymbus ternetzi
55 mm (2.25 in)
South America

The black colours of a shoal of these delightful small Tetras makes a welcome contrast in the aquarium. The large sooty-black anal fin together with the equally black rear half of the younger fish gives the fish its alternative popular name of Petticoat Fish. This coloration fades with age, the fish becoming a much less attractive grey. In recent years, there has been an aquarium-cultivated, long-finned variety introduced.

Glowlight Tetra
Hemigrammus erythrozonus
45 mm (1.75 in)
Guyana

A very beautiful fish, with a warm-glowing line running alont the top part of the body. Red appears in the front of the white-tipped dorsal and on the top half of the eye. The female is noticeably deeper-bodied than the male who, at times, can look decidedly 'hollow-bellied'. Spawning is possible, but the conditions must be carefully controlled as soft, acid water seems to bring the best results.

The delicate colours of the Glowlight Tetra, Hemigrammus erythrozonus, *may not be quite as strong as those of its near relatives, but a shoal of these fishes in a well-planted, quiet tank will look magnificent*

Rummy-nosed Tetra
Hemigrammus rhodostomus
55 mm (2.25 in)
Brazil

Two factors make this fish popular – its bright red nose and the black and white stripes on the caudal fin. Females are deeper-bodied. A similar-looking fish, *Petitella georgiae*, is slightly larger and telling the two species apart can be difficult: some reports dwell on slight differences in the caudal fin coloration and the amount of red on the head. Breeding this shy and sensitive fish may be difficult.

Lemon Tetra
Hyphessobrycon pulchripinnis
50 mm (2 in)
South America

A long-standing aquarium favourite, the Lemon Tetra has a delicate yellowish hue to the body. The front edges of the anal, dorsal and ventral fins are bright yellow backed up with black. The top half of the eye is bright scarlet. An albino form has been bred. Females can be recognized by their deeper, plumper bodies.

Above: Each end of the Rummy-nosed Tetra is attractive – bright red nose and black and white caudal fin
Below: The delicate colours of the Lemon Tetra

The red and black markings should make for reasonable identification of the Serpae Tetra, Hyphessobrycon serpae, *although there are a number of very similar-looking sub-species to confuse the issue*

Serpae Tetra
Hyphessobrycon serpae
45 mm (1.75 in)
South America

A vividly-coloured species, the Serpae Tetra comes from a group of very similar-looking, similarly-coloured fishes (*H. bentosi*, *H. callistus*, *H. minor*). Body colour is deep pink and there is a black patch at the fish's shoulder. Fins are black-edged with the dorsal having a large black blotch. The species has obtained a reputation as a fin-nipper, so care should be taken in choosing tankmates.

Blue Emperor
Inpaichthys kerri
50 mm (2 in)
South America

*Close examination of this species, the Blue Emperor (*Inpaichthys kerri*), will soon reveal the differences between it and the often confused Emperor Tetra,* Nematobrycon palmeri *(see page 60)*

At first sight, very similar to the Emperor Tetra, *Nematobrycon palmeri*, but closer examination will reveal several differences. The shape of the fins is different: the anal fin, although yellow, lacks the thin black decorative line and the caudal fin has rounded lobes. That of the male does not develop filaments from the tips and centre rays. The dorsal fin is more rounded than sickle-shaped. The body is also more stocky and all the two species really have in common is a dark blue-black band along the flanks. This is a recently introduced fish, and the generic name refers to a South American Ichthyological Institute; the specific name honours the ichthyologist Kerr. Spawning details are not known.

Red Phantom Tetra
Megalamphodus sweglesi
40 mm (1.5 in)
South America

This species, together with *M. megalopterus*, provides the aquarium with two colour versions of an otherwise identical fish. Both species are found in South America. The red coloration stands out well in a well planted aquarium.

The Red Phantom Tetra, Megalamphodus sweglesi, *is a very attractive fish, but for those hobbyists not wanting too much red in their tanks, there is an equally beautiful black version,* M. megalopterus

The true colours and sparkling scales of the Diamond Tetra, Moenkhausia pittieri, *will only be revealed to the full when sidelighting strikes the fish through the aquarium's front glass*

Diamond Tetra
Moenkhausia pittieri
65 mm (2.5 in)
Venezuela

An often neglected fish, probably overlooked for its apparent lack of vivid colour. However, see this fish in a little side-lighting and its principal attraction is revealed. The sparkling iridescence of its scales is provided by their reflective edges. The dorsal and anal fins are well-developed, particularly those of the male; another beautiful feature is that the fins are outlined in blue-white. Give the fish a well-furnished aquarium with dark green plants, some bogwood decoration and a dark peat-covered base and you will then see it to advantage. Can be bred in the aquarium.

Glass Tetra, Red Eye Tetra
Moenkhausia sanctaefilomenae
100 mm (4 in)
Brazil, Paraguay

A heavily-built fish, made to look more so by the dull grey coloration of the dark-edged scales. Vertical bands of yellow and black cross the caudal peduncle immediately ahead of the caudal fin itself. The top half of the eye is bright red. Females are deeper-bodied than males. Some reports say that soft-leaved plants may be at risk; some vegetable matter should be included in their diet. A similar species, *M. oligolepis*, is larger; if kept in hard water it is reported to increase the risk of tuberculosis.

The rather dull-grey coloration of the Glass Tetra, Moenkhausia sanctofilaemenae, *are alleviated slightly by the bright red eye and the yellow and black markings across the caudal peduncle*

Emperor Tetra
Nematobrycon palmeri
60 mm (2.5 in)
Colombia

A very striking fish, perhaps the most colourful of the species in the genus. The main features are the broad blue-black line running along the top part of the body, and the yellow fins. The anal fin is concave with a thin black-lined decoration running along its border. The male's dorsal fin is sickle-shaped and has a filamentous extension; similarly his caudal fin has filaments growing out from each tip and from the centre ray. The female does not have these extensions. A further way of sexing these fishes is to note the colour of the eye, those of the male being a different shade to the female, more blue than green. Spawning results in a small number of fry and although soft, acid water is said to give good results, breeding in hard water has been successfully achieved.

Cardinal Tetra
Paracheirodon axelrodi
45 mm (1.75 in)
South America

Despite having been around for many years, the Cardinal Tetra never fails to excite those seeing it for the first time. The scarlet band running the length of the bottom half of the body is topped by a band of electric blue. A shoal of these fishes in a well-planted aquarium almost defies description. Females are a little deeper in the body. Spawning has been regularly achieved in the aquarium.

The male Emperor Tetra, Nematobrycon palmeri *has a sickle-shaped dorsal fin and extended rays from the centre and edges of the caudal fin*

*The Cardinal Tetra (**opposite top**) has the edge on its near relative the Neon Tetra (**opposite bottom**) as far as the red coloration is concerned. The Cardinal's red area covers the whole lower half of the body, whereas the Neon Tetra's only reaches halfway along*

Neon Tetra
Paracheirodon innesi
42 mm (1.5 in)
South America

Until the discovery of the Cardinal Tetra, the Neon Tetra held pride of place as the most colourful Tetra. The main difference, apart from size, is that the red area only reaches halfway along the body. Again females are deeper-bodied and when filling with eggs may effectively put a 'bend' in the electric-blue line. Reports indicate that a slightly lower temperature, coupled with the use of young adults, provide the best results when breeding. Although originating in South America, most Neon Tetras now come from commercial breeders in the Far East – to such an extent that they are now becoming referred to as Hong Kong Tetras, replacing the Angelfish (another South American 'exile' also bred in similar commercial quantities) as the most popular aquarium fish.

Congo Tetra
Phenacogrammus interruptus
90 mm (3.5 in)
Zaire

Here is another shoaling fish whose white-outlined fins are seen to best advantage when kept in an aquarium furnished with dark green plants, bogwood and a dark-coloured base. The male fish displays a broad band of iridescent blue, green and gold along the flanks; like most African Characins, the scales are large and are well defined with darker edges. The dorsal and caudal fins are well-produced with long extensions, those in the caudal fin emerging from the centre rays. The female is browner and her caudal fin is straight-edged. The fish is an active swimmer, and requires a large aquarium. The eggs are quite large and after fertilization drop to the bottom and develop a hard outer covering as protection whilst the 6-day or so hatching period passes. This fish is often referred to as *Micralestes interruptus*.

X-ray Fish
Pristella maxillaris
45 mm (1.75 in)
South America

The main attraction of this fish is its almost complete transparency, only the internal body organs are hidden from view in a silvery sac. Anal, dorsal and ventral fins have black tips and the caudal fin is red. A small black spot appears behind the gill-cover. Male fishes have a more elongated internal organ sac than females. Formerly *P. riddlei*.

The Congo Tetra, Phenacogrammus interruptus, *has large scales like all African Characins but its main attraction is the turquoise blue-green and gold iridescences along the flanks of the male fish. He also has long extensions to the dorsal and caudal fins*

Right: The X-ray Fish, Pristella maxillaris, *is aptly named as the body looks quite transparent in places*

The Striped Headstander, Anostomus anostomus, *has a characteristic habit of resting with a head-down attitude*

Related Families

Striped Headstander
Anostomus anostomus
140 mm (5.5 in)
South America

The long pencil-like body has three dark bands running along its length, separated by gold. The dorsal and anal fins are red, the remainder being more yellow. A feature of this fish is its characteristic 'head down' position in the water, especially when at rest. The mouth is upward tilting (usually denoting a surface feeder) so this fish has to do some very acrobatic twisting to pick up food from the bottom of the aquarium. An aquarium furnished with thin canes to simulate reedbeds or planted with plenty of tall *Vallisneria* or *Sagittaria* growths will make this fish feel quite at home. The fish will graze on soft algae and if extra greenstuffs are not provided (blanched lettuce and spinach leaves are ideal) then attention may be turned to soft-leaved plants in the aquarium. Spawning details are not known.

The Marbled Hatchetfish, Carnegiella strigata, *is an expert leaper and the tank should be tightly-covered to prevent escapees*

Marbled Hatchetfish
Carnegiella strigata
65 mm (2.5 in)
South America

The Hatchetfishes are deep-bodied for a special reason. The increased depth accommodates the very powerful pectoral muscles which beat the pectoral fins like wings to propel the fish out of the water and several metres across the surface. A tight-fitting tank cover is essential for the security of all the Hatchetfishes. Insects, waterborne larvae and other live foods constitute a major part of the fish's diet in nature and these should also be provided in captivity. The lower half of the body of this species is covered with a marbled patterning, the area above a line from snout to the centre of the caudal fin is quite plain.

Spotted Headstander
Chilodus punctatus
80 mm (3.25 in)
South America

A smart-looking fish with clearly-defined scales each having a dark section at its front edge. The overall effect is to give the fish a dotted effect. The dorsal is square-shaped and also dotted with dark spots. A dark line runs from the uptilted snout through the centre of the eye to the caudal fin. Spawning occurs near to the bottom of the aquarium and weighted-down nylon mops can be provided to receive the eggs. The head-down swimming and resting position gives the fish its popular name.

Splashing Tetra, Spraying Characin
Copella arnoldi
110 mm (4.25 in)
South America

This fish has an almost Killifish-shaped body and the scales are dark-edged. A short dark line runs from the snout to just behind the gill-cover. Fins are yellowish-red, some with black margins. The dorsal has a black blotch above a small white area; the caudal fin is asymmetrical (the upper lobe being larger than the lower) and plays quite an important part in the unique reproductive behaviour. The smaller female lacks some of the reddish coloration but also has a similarly-decorated dorsal fin.

This species lays its fertilized eggs in a very safe place as far as protection from other fishes is concerned: in nature, it chooses the underside of an overhanging terrestrial plant above the water, well out of reach of any would be aquatic egg-stealer. In captivity the tank hood or the over-glass will be readily accepted as a substitute. The problem then is how to keep them from drying out during the 36 hours or so before hatching. Here the male's large caudal fin comes into play, for he continually splashes water onto the eggs to prevent them dehydrating. The youngsters eventually fall into the water and begin feeding on very small foods. The number of eggs in a brood ranges from 50 to 200. Often referred to as *Copeina arnoldi*.

Above: The Splashing Tetra, Copella arnoldi, *has developed a fool-proof system of protecting its eggs from the attention of other fish – it lays them out of water well out of their reach*

The Spotted Headstander, Chilodus punctatus, *is another fish with an oblique, 'head-down' attitude towards life*

Long-nosed Distichodus
Distichodus lusosso
330 mm (13 in)
Central Africa

Despite its size, this long-snouted fish has a peaceful disposition but naturally requires a very large aquarium for comfortable accommodation. The newly-emerging shoots of aquarium plants may be nibbled, so the aquarium should be furnished with wood or tree roots and the fish's dietary needs supplemented with wheatgerm flakes, rolled oats, lettuce and/or spinach leaves. No reports published on spawnings in captivity.

The sheer size of the spectacularly-marked Distichodus lussoso *precludes it from anything but the largest aquarium*

Spotted Hatchetfish
Gasteropelecus maculatus
95 mm (3.75 in)
South America

The area above the dark line running from snout to caudal fin is marked with spots. Below the horizontal line there are vertical rows of dark dots. The dorsal fin is dark-edged.

Silver Hatchetfish
Gasteropelecus levis
60 mm (2 in)
South America

The body shape conforms to the Hatchetfish group's norm, but an adipose fin is present in this genus. The area above the horizontal dark line running from gill cover to caudal fin is slightly lighter-coloured. A dark blotch appears at the base of the dorsal fin and a dark vertical bar may just be discernible at the extreme rear edge of the caudal peduncle. This species is difficult to distinguish from the Common Hatchetfish (*G. sternicla*).

The straight-topped contour of its body allows the Silver Hatchetfish, Gasteropelecus levis, *to lurk immediately below the surface of the water waiting for insects to come within jumping reach*

The Spotted Hatchetfish, Gasteropelecus maculatus, *has a deep body accommodating powerful pectoral fin muscles*

Spotted Leporinus
Leporinus maculatus
130 mm (5 in)
South America

The generic name *Leporinus* means 'hare-like' and is a reference to the shape of the fish's mouth which resembles that of a hare. Like the terrestrial animal, this genus also eats greenstuffs – only in this case it is more than likely to be the aquarium plants. Another safeguard is to keep the tank cover secure, for these fish (like all those in the genus) are agile jumpers. The body is not quite so streamlined as in other members of the genus; the sides are adorned with several large blotches.

Although itself attractively marked, the Spotted Leporinus, Leporinus maculatus, *will soon destroy the aquarium plants. Furnish the tank accordingly, using tough-leaved (or even plastic) plants*

The Golden Pencilfish, Nannostomus beckfordi, *has much to offer the hobbyist – it is hardy, beautiful and, given the correct conditions, will breed in the aquarium*

Golden Pencilfish
Nannostomus beckfordi
50 mm (2 in)
South America

The small Pencilfishes make delightful aquarium subjects. They are relatively active, with males constantly displaying to the females or threatening rivals. The golden area above the single horizontal stripe accounts for the fish's popular name. Although this is visually a 'One-line' Pencilfish, this popular name is better reserved for *N. unifasciatus*, a much more delicate fish. The scattered eggs are very susceptible to poor water conditions and will not develop even if fully fertilized.

The taxonomic classification of this family has been under almost constant revision. Lebiasinidae is its latest resting place, previous family names have included Hemiodontidae and Nannostomidae. At one time the generic names cited for different species now included in the genus *Nannostomus* were *Nannobrycon* and *Poecilobrycon*. The confusion (or more properly, the scientific debate) was due to the differences in behaviour in swimming attitudes, some species swimming and resting 'head-up', a situation not helped any further by the young of some species swimming at a slant before maturing into horizontal swimmers!

Dwarf Pencilfish
Nannostomus marginatus
38 mm (1.5 in)
South America

Perhaps the most beautiful of the Pencilfishes. The stocky body carries three horizontal lines (the lowest of the three is often hard to see being almost underneath the belly and not quite as long as the others). The dorsal, anal and ventral fins are red marked with black.

Males may have more red in their ventral fins. A very avid egg-eater so be sure to take the usual precautions to separate the fish from their eggs as soon as possible.

Three-banded Pencilfish
Nannostomus trifasciatus
50 mm (2 in)
South America

The three bands on the body of this species are much easier to see. The body is longer and although there is less red (but more blue) in the fins altogether, there are two red blotches in the caudal fin which also helps to distinguish this fish from the previous species. A delicate species and breeding can be difficult; this may be due in part again to adverse water conditions which prevent the eggs from developing properly.

Above: The Dwarf Pencilfish, Nannostomus marginatus, *is much sought after by fishkeepers as it makes an excellent shoaling fish for the smaller aquarium*

The Three-lined Pencilfish, Nannostomus trifasciatus, *is a larger more slender Pencilfish but equally adaptable to aquarium life*

Red Piranha, Red-bellied Piranha, Natterer's Piranha
Serrasalmus nattereri
300 mm (11.75 in)
South America

What can you say about the Piranha – except don't put your fingers in the tank! More reasonably, do take care when netting these fishes for apart from nipping the fingers they can leap out of the net quite easily. The dull grey colour of this fish is relieved by the red area of the throat which spreads along the ventral surface to the anal fin; additionally, there are many reflective scales scattered over the body which make the fish glitter attractively when seen in an advantageous light. Feed with raw fish or meat foods. A shoal of Piranhas in a large public aquarium is quite impressive – or terrifying, depending on whether you are a fishkeeper or not. This species is also known as *Rooseveltiella nattereri*.

Many hobbyists would be more alarmed than disappointed if the Red Piranha, Serrasalmus nattereri, *really lived up to its reputation*

CICHLIDS

Cichlids are found almost worldwide, especially in Africa, Central and South America. There are only two species (in a single genus) native to Asia.

Ranging in size from 50 mm to 300 mm plus (2 in to over 12 in), cichlids arouse strong feelings wherever they are seen. They can be regarded as both graceful and brutish – the Angelfish and the Oscar illustrate this perfectly; in the aquarium they can be peaceful or bullies. Many are tank-wreckers, no plant surviving their depredations. So what makes them so popular?

The range of size in the cichlids means that they can be accommodated in all sizes of tanks. African species are brilliantly coloured. Even the largest appear to recognize their owner and allow themselves to be hand-petted. But the main interest in these fishes is their method of reproduction.

All cichlids show the highest degree of parental care; their spawning ritual is a model of good parenthood. The egg-depositing species carefully clean a spawning site, and guard their fertilized eggs fearlessly against all comers, no matter what size. The young may be transferred several times to a new, freshly-cleaned site before they become free-swimming, and even then the parents' attention never flags. It is not unknown for cichlids to spawn again whilst still shepherding their previous brood. Many African species practise mouthbrooding, the female incubating the fertilized eggs in her mouth, to which the free-swimming young fish rapidly retreat when frightened.

Individual Species

Sheepshead Acara
Aequidens curviceps
75 mm (3 in)
South America

This small cichlid is ideal for the community aquarium. It is peaceful, not too shy and will spawn quite willingly. The male can be usually distinguished from the female by his longer, more pointed fins – the anal and dorsal fins are the best indicators. At spawning time, like all cichlids, a small tube (the *ovipositor*) extends from the vent of both fishes and this, together with site-cleaning activities, is a sure sign that spawning is imminent. It spawns on flat rocks in open areas and usually takes on parental responsibilities quite well after one or two false starts, where both parents may eat their young.

The modestly-sized, and perfectly-behaved, Sheepshead Acara, Aequidens curviceps, *is an ideal small cichlid for the community tank*

The Blue Acara, Aequidens pulcher, *although a firm favourite amongst fishkeepers, should not be trusted with smaller fishes*

Blue Acara
Aequidens pulcher
160 mm (6.25 in)
South America

A larger version of the above species, the Blue Acara has been an aquarium favourite for many years. The facial blue patterning is quite pronounced and the fins also carry some patterning. Although likely to be pugnacious with the onset of old age, and a little destructive of plants around spawning time, it is generally a peaceful fish but may find that shoal of small Neon Tetras just too tempting. Spawns on flat horizontal surfaces in open areas and are usually excellent parents.

Agassiz's Dwarf Cichlid
Apistogramma agassizi
70 mm (2.75 in)
South America

The spade-shaped, white-bordered caudal fin is an umistakable guide to identification. Unfortunately, this only holds good for the male as many female *Apistogramma* species resemble each other, being golden brown with an oblique dark bar through the eye. A secretive spawner, most hobbyists find that a flowerpot laid on its side is accepted as an ideal substitute for a cave; after spawning occurs the female guards the eggs, viciously driving away the male and any other fish that ventures too near.

Agassiz's Dwarf Cichlid, Apistogramma agassizi, *is a secretive spawner and will not always let you see the whole breeding sequence*

Oscar
Astronotus ocellatus
280 mm (11 in)
South America

A large (and beautiful to its devotees) fish which has a tendency to play havoc with a neat and tidy tank. Being a hearty eater it inevitably produces plenty of waste material, and so an efficient filtration system is needed. It also has a healthy dislike of aquarium plants (which it will take great delight in uprooting, although it does not eat them) so rocky decorations are more practical. It redeems itself by becoming tame, recognizing its owner and allowing hand-stroking. Eggs numbering well in excess of 1000 are laid on flat firm surfaces and this output can be considered normal for a spawning. Several colour forms are seen, the original dark grey body colour with orange-ringed black blotches, the completely red-sided, black-finned, and the 'Tiger' variant, a mixture of black and red. As a young fish, the coloration is a pleasant marbling but do not be misled into thinking that the fish will stay either this size or this colour.

The Orange Chromide, Etroplus maculatus, *is a brightly-coloured fish which lays equally highly-coloured eggs*

Orange Chromide
Etroplus maculatus
90 mm (3.5 in)
India, Sri Lanka

Almost the sole representative of the cichlid group in Asia, the Orange Chromide has much to recommend it. Of medium size, the coloration is a rich orange/red covered in rows of tiny red spots and a black area on the flanks just above the anal fin. Females have white spots on the caudal fins. Spawning occurs in caves (again use flowerpots to simulate natural sites) and the eggs are orange. A larger green form, *Etroplus suratensis*, is the other species in this genus.

*Do not be tempted to buy the attractively-marked young Marbled Cichlid or Oscar (*Astronotus ocellatus*), unless you are prepared to put up with the large gluttonous fish that it grows into, in a very short space of time*

The Firemouth Cichlid, Heros meeki, *has an appearance that belies its actual character. It is generally a very peaceful fish despite its usually 'angry' expression*

Opposite: The African genus Julidochromis *provides several very attractively-marked species for the hard-water aquarium. This is* Julidochromis ornatus

Firemouth Cichlid
Heros meeki
150 mm (6 in)
South America

Despite its name and sometimes angry appearance, the Firemouth Cichlid is a relatively peaceful species although some rivalry may arise between males. The red area beneath the throat is limited to males and intensifies at breeding time when his dorsal and caudal fins develop extensions. One characteristic that does not always endear this fish to its owner is that of sometimes rearranging the contours of the gravel as it looks for food. Because of the interest in cichlids, their scientific classification appears to be under almost constant review and upheaval; this species has not been unaffected, the current generic name *Heros* taking over from the original *Cichlasoma* and even more recent *Thorichthys*.

Julidochromis ornatus
75 mm (3 in)
Africa

The cylindrical body is typical of the genus *Julidochromis*, and it allows the fish easy access to crevices in rocks. The aquarium should be furnished with plenty of caves, flowerpots and other retreat-forming structures. Spawning also occurs in caves. This species, as with other members of the genus, can be kept in quite small tanks but they can be upset by water change so the hobbyist must ensure that the filtration system deals efficiently with the disposal of ammonia. They are excellent leapers so keep the tank cover on securely.

African lake cichlids are very colourful. This is the Red-finned Cichlid, Labeotropheus trewavasae

Lamprologus brichardi *has a lyre-shaped caudal fin and white edges to all its fins. It spawns in caves and other similar secret sites*

Red-finned Cichlid
Labeotropheus trewavasae
150 mm (6 in)
Africa

The lakes of the African Rift Valley provided the hobby in general, and cichlid-fanciers in particular, with a great increase of interest a few years ago. The rock-dwelling cichlids of the shallower inshore waters were not only brightly-coloured but also thrived extremely well in hard water. Fishes of the mbuna group are rock grazing algae eaters, their top lip being specially adapted for this purpose.

Named in honour of Dr. Ethelwynne Trewavas, a famous ichthyologist at London's British Museum (Natural History), is another mbuna which, like all mbunas, is only found in Lake Malawi. Again, there are various colour 'morphs' and, whilst the normal male is blue with a red dorsal fin, the female is a mottled orange and black colour.

Lyretail Lamprologus
Lamprologus brichardi
80 mm (3.25 in)
Africa

A very beautiful fish from Lake Tanganyika that continued the impetus of interest started by other African lake cichlids. The fins are white-edged and the blue eye and facial markings contrast strongly with the surrounding dark markings and the bright yellow/gold spot immediately behind the gill-cover. Eggs are laid in caves, upside-down on the ceiling and whilst the young are relatively slow-growing, the parents will not let this surrounding brood stop them from producing even more youngsters. In sufficiently large aquariums several pairs can set up family territories without constant squabbling occurring. Of the genus, *Lamprologus brichardi* is probably the most peaceful, other members being physically much larger lake fishes, with distinctly anti-social habits, taking other fishes as food without any hesitation.

Festive Cichlid, Festivum
Mesonauta festivus
150 mm (6 in)
South America

An often neglected species but one well worth keeping. It has a very smart appearance, with a dark line slanting upwards from the snout, through the eye to the rear tip of the dorsal fin. The ventral fins are very similar in structure to those of the Angelfish (*Pterophyllum* sp.) whose native waters this fish shares. It spawns in the typical, well-caring cichlid manner, guarding its eggs and subsequent young with vigour and enthusiasm. The scientific name has recently been revised, older literature citing *Cichlasoma festivum* as the correct nomenclature.

The Festive or Flag Cichlid, Mesonauta festivus, *has long thin ventral fins similar to those of the Angelfish*

The Ram, Microgeophagus ramirezi, *is a very colourful dwarf cichlid but may prove to be a little delicate until you find the water conditions which suit it best*

Ram
Microgeophagus ramirezi
70 mm (2.75 in)
South America

Here is a beautiful fish, a fact with which everyone agrees, but with a series of names with which everyone appears to disagree! Originally named *Apistogramma ramirezi* the next favoured name was *Papiliochromis ramirezi.* There are two colour forms, the natural one with more vertical dark bands than the golden form, although both have gorgeous violet iridescence on the flanks. The first few rays of the dorsal fin are black and any sign of elongation of the second or third rays is usually taken as a sign of masculinity. Spawning occurs in a shallow depression dug in the gravel. Rams are somewhat delicate, requiring soft water, but experienced aquarists start them off in soft water which gradually hardens (by the action of normally calcium-rich gravel); further partial water replacement, using harder water, slowly acclimatizes the fish to domestic water conditions (unless you are fortunate enough to live in a soft water area) and subsequent generations can be reared in hard water straight from hatching.

The Kribensis, Pelvicachromis pulcher, *is a long-established aquarium favourite and usually proves to be both prolific and very good parents into the bargain*

Kribensis
Pelvicachromis pulcher
100 mm (4 in)
West Africa

A very popular species with hobbyists. A secretive spawner, which often retreats from sight for some days to emerge later complete with free-swimming brood. A certain amount of digging occurs but the fish may accept a flowerpot instead of ruining your aquatic scene. Preponderance of one sex in broods is quite common; reports suggest that alterations in water chemistry may reverse the imbalance.

Angelfish
Pterophyllum scalare
100 mm (4 in)
South America

It would be difficult to describe the Angelfish in any new way, such has been the literature devoted to this enormously popular cichlid. In addition to the 'standard' fish with the familiar black and silver markings, there are now many cultivated variants – all-black, half-black, marbled, gold, zebra (extra number of stripes), 'ghost' etc. Alongside these colour varieties there are also veiltail and lace fin variants. It is a good idea to wait until the newly set-up aquarium has become well-established (in water quality and nitrite levels) before introducing Angelfish as they can be susceptible to both 'new' water and rapidly-changing nitrite levels. Many educated guesses have been made as to sexing methods (lip-shapes, dorsal ray formation, angles of fin emergence, internal swim-bladder outlines etc.) but the best guide is to observe the shape of the breeding tube extended by each fish at spawning time; that of the female is much broader and blunter than the male's. An alternative method is to view the fish head-on. The male's cross-section is equally-symmetrical about the point of emergence of the pectoral fins: the female continues to increase in thickness well past this point and then tapers in rapidly.

Spawning is typical of open-water, substrate-spawners. A near-vertical firm surface is cleaned and other nearby fish chased away; eggs are first laid by the female followed by a fertilizing run over the egg-laden site by the male. Once hatched, the eggs remain fixed to the site by sticky threads and water is constantly fanned over the eggs by the parents, using their pectoral fins. Any dirt is removed from the eggs by the simple expedient of the parents picking up the eggs, chewing them, then re-depositing them back on the site, or another pre-cleaned one. (Fainthearted hobbyists should not watch, until the fishes are trusted not to eat their young!) This procedure is repeated until the free-swimming stage is reached, usually around 8–10 days after the eggs are laid, but even then the parents' task is not over. They shepherd their fry around the tank and at night the fry are stuck back on to yet another pre-cleaned site. You will see all this better if you give the parents a separate tank to spawn in. Having this family scene enacted in your own aquarium, whether it be Angelfish or any other parental-caring cichlid, is one of the best reasons for fishkeeping.

However, it is often regrettable, and annoying, that cichlids do not rear their young 'as per the book', and in this case the eggs should be removed from the parents and raised artificially. An air-stone placed by the egg-laden rock or leaf will assist waterflow over the eggs, and a little bactericide added to the water will prevent fungus forming on the eggs. (Methylene blue is often used but may be difficult to obtain.) Partial water changes will also help to keep the water pure (do not use fresh tapwater) and once the fry are free-swimming newly-hatched brine shrimp will get them off to a good start.

Since the introduction of the original 'standard' black-striped silver Angelfish, there have been many more aquarium-developed strains added to their numbers, most originating in fish-breeding stations in the Far East – thousands of miles away from the fish's natural home in the River Amazon

The Discus, or Pompadour Fish, Symphysodon *sp, is considered by some to be the ultimate freshwater fish to keep. It needs special care, whilst breeding is also not quite as straightforward as that of other cichlids*

Discus, Pompadour Fish
Symphysodon discus
150 mm (6 in)
South America

For some tropical freshwater fish-keepers, the keeping and breeding of Discus is the pinnacle of their hobby. The fishes are magnificent, there are several subspecies which exhibit their own particular colours and markings and, like the preceding species the breeding behaviour is spectacular. It follows the normal pattern until the fry are free-swimming and then a further development occurs: the young fish initially feed on a mucus secreted by their parents and this makes artificial rearing difficult should this prove necessary, although an American Discus-breeder, Jack Wattley, has developed a successful method for doing this.

COBITIDS (Loaches)

Resembling catfish in their bottom-dwelling habits, Loaches come in a variety of body shapes ranging from pencil-like to a more normal, albeit flat-bottomed shape. All have barbels and very tiny scales which give the appearance of naked skin. They can utilize atmospheric air in a similar manner to catfishes. Members of the genus *Botia* have erectile spines beneath the eye which act as a defensive mechanism (and can get caught in nets). Some are susceptible to changes in barometric pressure, becoming very active and making repeated dashes to the surface during periods of low pressure; this activity often precedes thunderstorms and one species in particular has predictably attracted the common name of Weatherfish. All are exceptionally fond of worm foods, which tend to draw them out from their resting places like a magnet.

Individual species

Coolie Loach
Acanthophthalmus kuhli
110 mm (4.25 in)
South-east Asia

Although the black-banded orange/ yellow bodies are attractive, this fish is not very often seen swimming about the aquarium. It is a nocturnal species and also limits its activities to wriggling round the plant bases looking for food. The standard number of fins are also present but they are very small and consequently hard to see. One thing is sure, they are hard to catch. Breeding has been reported in captivity and, true to nature, it appears to be a very tangled affair.

The Kuhli Loach, Acanthophthalmus kuhli, *seems to take a pride in tangling itself around the stems of aquarium plants – especially when you want to catch it*

The Clown Loach, Botia macracantha, *is the most colourful and largest species in the* Botia *genus*

Clown Loach
Botia macracantha
300 mm (12 in)
South-east Asia

This very smart-looking black and orange fish is popular with hobbyists but is often purchased to be the sole representative of its species in the aquarium. Clown Loaches are very gregarious fishes and usually thrive much better when kept in small shoals. The scales are very small, giving the fish a naked appearance. Although they grow to a good size in the wild, domestic aquarium species hardly ever reach these proportions and a two-thirds size specimen may be regarded as a prizewinning example. They may be intolerant to disease remedies.

Chained Loach
Botia sidthimunki
55 mm (2.25 in)
South-east Asia

Whilst most loaches are nocturnal, the Chained Loach is reasonably active during the daytime. It ventures higher in the water than most, often perching on broad leaves to rest and survey the underwater scene. It should be kept in a quiet aquarium with fishes of its own size.

The Chained Loach, Botia sidthimunki, *spends a lot of its time swimming in midwater areas of the aquarium*

CYPRINIDS

The Cyprinid family contains in the region of 1500 species found almost worldwide. Sizes vary considerably, ranging from 25 mm (1 in) to over 1 metre (40 in plus) but aquarium specimens are generally of modest size. They are hardy, active fishes and a large proportion are willing to breed in captivity.

Cyprinids occupy all levels of the water. Barbs (so-called because of the barbels around the mouth), spend most of their time foraging around the bottom; large species are apt to stir up detritus, so efficient filtration is necessary to keep the water clear and clean. Rasboras tend to occupy the mid- and upper levels and, together with the surface-swimming Danios, add activity to the aquarium. All acclimatize to domestic water supplies easily. Cyprinids have no teeth in the mouth but use pharyngeal teeth to grind up their food.

Cyprinids are promiscuous, males breeding spontaneously with any ripe female of the same species. Many, especially Danios, can be spawned collectively as a shoal. In general, reproduction is by egg-scattering although a few cyprinids are egg-depositors.

To breed cyprinids successfully in captivity, their notorious egg-eating habits must be curbed. Bushy plants such as *Elodea*, *Ceratophyllum* and *Myriophyllum* in the breeding tank make good egg-traps. Alternatively, spawn the fish above a fine net suspended in the water, or over a base-covering of glass marbles. These methods effectively deny the parents access to their fertilized eggs.

Like all aquarium fishes, cyprinids will fall foul of the usual fish ailments. Indeed, some species are good indicators of aquarium hygiene, often exhibiting symptoms well before the other occupants. The Black Ruby Barb, *Barbus nigrofasciatus*, is a good example.

Barbs

Clipper Barb
Barbus callipterus
90 mm (3.5 in)
West Africa

The large scales and coloration of this fish are similar to the African Characin *Arnoldichthys spilopterus* but the two can be easily distinguished for the Characin has the small extra adipose fin. The dorsal fin is marked with black. Little is known about its reproductive behaviour.

The Clipper Barb, Barbus callipterus, *is an African species and has large scales like many fishes from that continent*

The deep coppery-red colour of the male Rosy Barb, Barbus conchonius, *at breeding time is but one attraction of this hardy fish*

Rosy Barb
Barbus conchonius
75 mm (3 in)
North-east India

The rosy silvery-bronze hue of the male fish turns into a deep coppery red at spawning time. Another clue to sexing this fish is that the male has darker fins. A very prolific fish and one that is easy to breed in the aquarium. A longer-finned variety has been developed, as the result of intensive selective breeding programmes.

Cuming's Barb, Barbus cumingi, *is a single species collected in Sri Lanka and there appear to be two distinct physical forms – one with red fins, one with orange-yellow fins*

The Clown Barb, Barbus everetti, *has the same red/orange black coloration as the Clown Loach but, of course, is not related*

Cuming's Barb
Barbus cumingi
50 mm (2 in)
Sri Lanka

Two dark spots on a silver body is not an uncommon coloration for fishes in general nor of Barbs in particular. However, the associated yellow fins in this case make for easy identification. There is also a variety that carries more reddish fins but this is merely a colour-variant from another location and not a separate species.

Clown Barb
Barbus everetti
140 mm (5.5 in)
Malaya, Borneo

The orange and black bars on the body make this fish instantly recognizable. It does like vegetable matter in its diet, so the aquarium should be planted with stout-leaved (or plastic) plants if you want your natural aquarium decorations to survive!

The Dwarf Golden Barb, Barbus gelius, *is an ideal fish for the smaller, fully-furnished aquarium*

Opposite: The Spanner Barb, Barbus lateristriga, *is a large Barb that loses some of its well-defined markings as it gets older*

Dwarf Golden Barb
Barbus gelius
38 mm (1.5 in)
Indo-China, Bengal

This delightful small Barb, its yellow body marked with black, may escape your notice in dealers' tanks. It needs a well-planted, quiet aquarium where it can overcome its shyness. Its natural habitat has conditioned it to withstand slightly cooler conditions than those required by its more colourful relatives.

Spanner Barb, 'T' Barb
Barbus lateristriga
160 mm (6.25 in)
Indonesia, Malaya, Thailand

The black markings on a pale pink background are similar to the profile of an adjustable spanner, or wrench. Where one of the two crosspieces are missing then the alternative common name is more apt. This large fish is peaceful when small but may bother smaller fishes when fully grown. The coloration is not so distinct with increasing age and the fish become less attractive.

The male Ruby Barb, Barbus nigrofasciatus, *turns from a black-banded fish into a spectacular deep-red, purple-headed wonder at breeding time*

Black, Ruby or Purple-headed Barb
Barbus nigrofasciatus
60 mm (2.25 in)
Sri Lanka

A well-described fish, for the head of the male becomes suffused with a deep rich purple-red at spawning times. Normal coloration is a yellow/gold body crossed by wide dark vertical bands. The male's fins are black, the female's clear. A normally hardy community fish, the Ruby Barb appears to contract white spot disease ahead of the other aquarium inmates, and although the fish recovers quite rapidly with efficient medication, this can prove to be good advance warning of impending trouble.

Odessa Barb
Barbus 'odessa'
60 mm (2.25 in)

A relatively recently-introduced fish which has proved to be both colourful and a prolific breeder. The main feature is the horizontal broad band of vivid red along its flanks. Its origins are clouded in mystery. It may be an aquarium-developed strain of a single species or it may be a hybrid of other species (including *B.ticto*). It is said to have been introduced into the hobby via the Ukrainian port of Odessa.

The Odessa Barb, Barbus 'odessa', *may still not be positively identified from the scientific point of view, but it is a real favourite with fishkeepers*

Checker or Island Barb
Barbus oligolepis
45 mm (1.75 in)
Sumatra

The sparkling scales of this fish are dark-edged giving a chequered pattern. The anal, caudal and dorsal fins of the male are red with black edgings, the female's fins are plain coloured.

Above: The Checker Barb has dark-edged scales which makes them very easy to see

Left: The Schuberti Barb is another fish with a little mystery surrounding its actual origins

Below: The Tinfoil Barb is a real show-stopper in its adult size and sparkling coloration

Schuberti Barb
Barbus 'schuberti'
75 mm (3 in)

Another fish of unknown origin. Physically, although of a gold colour, it bears a strong similarity to the more normally coloured *B. semifasciolatus* the Half-striped or Green Barb from China. It was possibly aquarium-developed from a xanthic (yellow) sport.

Tinfoil or Goldfoil Barb
Barbus schwanenfeldi
300 mm (11.75 in)
Indonesia, Malaya, Thailand

A very large fish, the Tinfoil is *the* Barb for the exhibition or public aquarium. A pretty fish, even when small, it grows rapidly and relishes vegetable matter in its diet so a planted aquarium can be denuded of soft-leaved plants very quickly. Obviously, this species requires very spacious accommodation in which to thrive.

Tiger Barb
Barbus tetrazona
65 mm (2.25 in)
Sumatra, Borneo

A very popular aquarium fish with a reputation for nipping the fins of slower-moving fishes. However, keeping them in a shoal will lessen this tendency, which may arise out of boredom or loneliness. The male's red colours intensify at spawning time. Various colour strains have been aquarium-developed – green, albino etc.

Ticto or Two-spot Barb
Barbus ticto
90 mm (3.5 in)
Sri Lanka

A very beautiful fish with a red and black patterned dorsal fin. Can withstand slightly cooler water. There are similar fishes (*B. stoliczkanus* and *B. phutunio*) which have been classed as separate or subspecies alongside this fish, and although they are very similar have slight physical differences – a smaller number of scales or an incomplete lateral line for instance.

Like all members of the genus, the Ticto Barb, Barbus ticto, *combines hardiness with popularity. In short an ideal aquarium subject*

Below: Despite its small proportions, the Cherry Barb, Barbus titteya, *will brighten up any community collection with its brilliant colours*

Cherry Barb
Barbus titteya
45 mm (1.75 in)
Sri Lanka

A cherry-red fish, ideally-suited to a well-planted small aquarium. The female is less brilliantly coloured having a browner hue. The male's colours intensify at spawning time.

Left: Tiger Barbs, Barbus tetrazona, *make an extremely colourful and active addition to the aquarium*

The Pearl Danio, Brachydanio albolineatus, *combines a very delicate coloration with constant activity around the upper levels of the tank*

Danios

Pearl Danio
Brachydanio albolineatus
55 mm (2.25 in)
South-east Asia

The coloration is most subtle, the pearly sheen constantly varying as the light catches the sides of this active fish. A shoal looks quite spectacular, especially in morning sunshine. Females take on a heavier appearance when filled with eggs prior to spawning.

The Leopard Danio, Brachydanio frankei, *appears to be an aquarium-developed fish rather than one found in the wild; the long-finned variety shown here is definitely so*

Leopard Danio
Brachydanio frankei
55 mm (2.25 in)
Thailand perhaps

The slight doubt as to the actual origins of this fish is because there is little record of it occurring in nature. It is probably an aquarium-developed strain from a cross involving *B. rerio.*

Zebra Danio
Brachydanio rerio
50 mm (2 in)
Eastern India

The body is covered with longitudinal alternate blue and silver/gold stripes, which extend into the fins of the male; these horizontal lines accentuate the fish's slimness. If you look closely at the head, you will see two pairs of barbels around the mouth which, although usually indicative of a bottom-feeding fish, is not the case in this instance as the fish spends most of the time actively swimming in the upper layers of the water. This species is an ideal aquarium subject being hardy, long-lived, easy to feed and to breed.

One of the most popular Danios and certainly an ideal fish to use as an introduction to an egglaying-species breeding programme. Sexing the fish is easy; males retain their slimness whilst the females noticeably fill out with eggs. After segregating the sexes for two weeks, placing the two fish (or even a shoal) together again usually results in hectic spawning behaviour. Precautions must be taken to safeguard the eggs as the parents are avid egg-eaters.

The favourite Zebra Danio, Brachydanio rerio, *is very hardy and very easy to breed. A long-finned variety has also been developed by selective breeding*

The Giant Danio, Danio aequipinnatus, *needs plenty of swimming space, for it is both a large fish and constantly on the move*

Giant Danio
Danio aequipinnatus (malabaricus)
100 mm (4 in)
India, Sri Lanka

One of the largest Danios, the coloration is not dissimilar to that of the Zebra Danio but the stripes are fewer and wider, with the gold or yellow much more apparent. There are also one or two vertical yellow lines just behind the gill cover. This very active species obviously requires space in which to exercise but fortunately, like most Danios, its surface-swimming tendency does help to keep it out of the other fishes' way.

Rasboras

Harlequin Fish
Rasbora heteromorpha
45 mm (1.75 in)
Borneo, Malaya, Indonesia

Despite belonging to the Cyprinid family, the Harlequin Fish does not share the characteristic pattern of reproduction. Eggs are deposited on the undersides of broad-leaved plants rather than being haphazardly scattered; however, parental care is not exercised. The degree of definition of the blue/black triangle on the side can be a useful guide to the sex of the fish: that on the male fish is clearly defined with sharp points whereas that of the female may become more blurred, particularly on the rear lower portion. A slimmer, more elongated species, *R. hengeli* is similarly marked and a fish of the same body shape, but lacking the triangular marking entirely, is *R. vaterifloris*.

Spotted, Dwarf or Pigmy Rasbora
Rasbora maculata
25 mm (1 in)
Indonesia, Malaya

One of the smallest fishes to be kept in the aquarium, the Spotted Rasbora is exactly named. In addition to the small dark spots on the body the red fins are also marked with black. Care must be taken when choosing tankmates for this species – similar-sized fishes will not intimidate it. Alternatively, a modestly-sized but well-planted aquarium will make an excellent home for a small shoal of these fishes. Because of their diminutive size, spawning may be prob-

lematical: numbers of young will be small and because of their size may present initial feeding problems.

Above: The triangular marking on the sides make identification of the Harlequin Fish, Rasbora heteromorpha, *very easy*

The Spotted Rasbora, Rasbora maculata, *is one of the smallest aquarium fishes*

The Scissortail, Rasbora trilineata, *may not always be on the move swimming-wise, but the lobes of the caudal fin never rest*

Scissortail
Rasbora trilineata
100 mm (4 in)
Malaya

From one extreme to another. This fish is one of the largest in the genus. It takes its common name from the habit of constantly twitching its well-marked caudal fin. The 'three-lined' description of the specific name also takes into consideration the third marking, a thin black line along the centre of the body, but it is the two black lobes of the caudal fin that seems to have attracted all the attention. This fish should be provided with plenty of swimming space. There is a similar species, *R. caudimaculata*, which has orange and black-coloured lobes to its equally-restless caudal fin.

Opposite: The very smart-looking Silver Shark, Balantiocheilus melanopterus, *is a rapidly-growing fish and constantly active in the aquarium*

Other Cyprinids

Silver Shark
Balantiocheilus melanopterus
350 mm (14 in)
Borneo, Sumatra, Thailand

A striking fish with black-edged fins contrasting sharply with the silver body. A fast-growing species that is constantly active in the aquarium. Another species that looks good in a shoal, you will need a large aquarium to accommodate even a small number of them.

Flying Fox
Epalzeorhynchus kallopterus
140 mm (5.5 in)
Borneo, Indonesia

The two horizontal dark stripes are divided by a yellow-gold band and make this active species a very smart-looking addition to the aquarium. It often rests perched on its anal and ventral fins on the surfaces of broad-leaved plants, rocks or logs. It will appreciate some vegetable matter in its diet. Peaceful towards other fish but may quarrel with other members of its species.

The Flying Fox, Epalzeorhynchus kallopterus, *often can be seen perched on a broad-leaved plant having a rest from its exertions*

The Sucking Loach has a reputation for being an eater of algae but you must also expect it to get a little aggressive when older

Opposite, top: The White Cloud Mountain Minnow is a colourful fish which can be kept outdoors in small pools during the summer

Opposite, below: The Red-tailed Black Shark has become a firm favourite due both to its striking coloration and no little imagination on the part of the fishkeeper

Sucking 'Loach', Chinese Algae-eater
Gyrinocheilus aymonieri
250 mm (10 in)
Thailand

This species is neither a loach nor, as its alternative name suggests, does it come from China. It does eat a certain amount of algae (particularly when young) but with increasing age it may pester slower swimming species who venture into its chosen territory. A special feature of this fish is the extra hole above each gill-cover which allows the fish to continue breathing whilst still clinging to the rocks with its specially adapted underslung mouth.

Red-tailed Black 'Shark'
Labeo bicolor
150 mm (6 in)
Thailand

A very popular fish, but not related to real sharks in any way. The name is based on the appearance of the dorsal fin which many fishkeepers associate with the marine fish. It often decides that a certain area of the tank is exclusively his (or hers – sexing is difficult) and turns aggressive towards intruders.

White Cloud Mountain Minnow
Tanichthys albonubes
45 mm (1.75 in)
China

Tales of discovery can be no more romantic than in this case, where the fish was found by a Chinese Boy Scout called Tan in the White Cloud Mountains. The colours can be very brilliant, the fins tipped with yellow and the iridescent line along the body resembling that of the Neon Tetra to some degree. This fish can be kept outdoors in ponds during warm summer months and need not necessarily be kept at such high temperatures as other tropical species. A long-finned variety has been developed.

CYPRINODONTIDS

(Killifishes)

Also known by the less tongue-tying names of Egglaying Toothcarps or Killifish, these miniature pike-like fishes from South America, Africa and parts of Asia are brilliantly coloured. Many can be kept in unheated aquariums, or at temperatures slightly below that expected for tropical fishes generally. Due to their pugnacity, it is normal to keep only a pair or trio of fishes together, and this can be done quite adequately in much smaller tanks.

Some Killifishes (the name means nothing more sinister than 'ditch-fishes') inhabit jungle streams which generally dry up each year. They have evolved a special method of reproduction to ensure that the young fry continue the family even though they themselves die as their watercourses evaporate.

Fertilized eggs are laid in the bottom mud and lie dormant until the next period of rain fills the streambed again. This triggers hatching and the young fry emerge to take full advantage of the extra food swept into the water by the rains. Even though Killifishes may live longer in captivity they are still very short-lived but their reproductive activity is well worth studying.

Depending on species, eggs may be laid in clumps of plants (synthetic nylon 'wool' mops can be substituted) or in a deep layer of peat-fibre on the bottom of the tank. Plant- or mop-deposited eggs can be removed to water in a shallow container kept in a warm place to hatch. Eggs laid in peat require semi-drying (gently squeeze the peat to remove most of the water) followed by a few weeks or even months storage in a plastic bag. Re-immersing the egg-laden peat after the required period has elapsed will activate the eggs into hatching. Nature has one further trick up her sleeve – sometimes the first rainfall does not last long enough to fill the streambed; so one immersion may not trigger the eggs and a second attempt should be made which is usually effective.

The Lyretailed Panchax, Aphyosemion australe, *is brilliantly-coloured like all members of the genus*

Individual Species

Lyretailed Panchax
Aphyosemion australe
60 mm (2.5 in)
West Africa

The golden brown body is covered with dark red specks. The single fins have red borders edged with yellow, and the caudal fin has extensions giving it the lyretail shape. The female is less colourful, and smaller. Spawning occurs in mops (substituting for bushy plants) and the removed eggs will hatch in shallow water in two weeks or so. Can be kept at relatively low temperatures in small well-planted aquariums. As the male chases the female vigorously during spawning, it may be better to spread the attention of the amorous male by using two or three females.

Red Lyretail
Aphyosemion bivittatum
60 mm (2.5 in)
West Africa

The *bivittatum* group has well over a dozen separate colour variants; each coming from a specific area. Like most Killifishes, the aquarium need not be large nor too brightly lit. This fish is also a mop-spawner. Females are smaller and less colourful.

Steel-blue Aphyosemion
Aphyosemion gardneri
70 mm (2.75 in)
West Africa

The natural distribution of this species has produced another popular group with several colour variants depending on areas of collection. The differences are generally limited to the coloration of the fin borders. The females are always smaller and less colourful. The fish follows the mop-spawning method of reproduction.

Aphyosemion gardneri *has several colour variants, the colour patterning depending on where the fish was collected*

Aphysosemion bivittatum *is another species with several colour forms. It takes a specialist Killifish-keeper to differentiate positively between them*

The Blackfinned Pearlfish, Cynolebias nigripinnis, *needs a deep layer of peat fibre on the aquarium floor in which to spawn*

Blackfinned Pearlfish
Cynolebias nigripinnis
50 mm (2 in)
Argentina, Paraguay, Uruguay

A genuine 'annual' species, the Blackfinned Pearlfish is an egg-burier. A deep layer of peat fibre on the floor of the aquarium makes a good spawning medium. The male's blue coloration deepens almost to black during spawning. The female is brownish and much smaller. This fish does well in a 'single species' aquarium set up to its own requirements. The eggs need storing for several months before attempts are made to activate hatching by re-immersion.

American Flagfish
Jordanella floridae
70 mm (2.75 in)
Florida

A much stockier-bodied fish, which takes its common name from the resemblance of the red stripes on its sides to the American flag; the fins of the male also have red patterning in them. Females lack the red coloration of the males but have a dark spot on the rear part of the dorsal fin. The dark spot midway along the body may sometimes be indistinct. Spawns in fine-leaved plants or may dig a depression in the gravel in which to deposit eggs. Whichever method is used, the female should be removed after spawning has ceased. The male will guard the eggs until hatching occurs – around 10 days or so. An aquarium with a good growth of soft green algae is appreciated. May be pugnacious to other fishes.

The American Flagfish, Jordanella floridae, *eats soft green algae and may spawn in a similar fashion to cichlids*

Guenther's Nothobranch
Nothobranchius guentheri
75 mm (3 in)
East Africa

Another spectacularly coloured species, again one best kept as a single species group. Males are quarrelsome so one male with a small 'harem' of females is the best arrangement. The scales are red-edged making each one quite distinct. Females of the *Nothobranchius* genus are all smaller than their mates, similar to each other and drably coloured; this makes positive identification difficult. Obtaining stock (or eggs) from specialist Killifish keepers or through the various International Killifish Associations will ensure correct pair selection. The fish is a substrate spawner, but the fish do not dive completely into the peat fibre but lay and fertilize eggs before physically embedding them into the top layer of the peat. They are often referred to as 'ploughers.' Some reports suggest that not all *Nothobranchius* eggs require dry storage and that keeping them in shallow water will suffice. However, the eggs still require six weeks or longer to mature before hatching occurs.

Guenther's Nothobranch, Nothobranchius guentheri, *is a very beautiful fish well worthy of the specialist care it needs*

Following spawning, the female Ricefish, Oryzias latipes, *drags around a clump of fertilized eggs hanging from her vent until they are brushed off onto the aquarium plants to hatch*

Medaka, Ricefish
Oryzias latipes
45 mm (1.75 in)
Japan

This small fish from the ricefields of Japan is a simple gold/yellow colour but has an interesting method of reproduction. Following the spawning chase and embrace, the fertilized eggs hang like a bunch of grapes from the female's vent until brushed off as the fish swims through the aquarium plants. As the fish naturally inhabits waters liable to be flooded by tidal actions, it can tolerate some salt in the water or other changing water conditions.

Playfair's Panchax
Pachypanchax playfairi
90 mm (3.5 in)
East Africa

An aggressive species that is very prolific in the aquarium. It spawns regularly in dense plants (a thick floating layer of *Riccia* makes an excellent spawning medium and provides a hiding place for the young fishes afterwards). A physical feature of this fish is the tendency of the scales to stand out from the body; although this may suggest an outbreak of dropsy to the worried beginner, there is no need to be alarmed – it is a perfectly natural phenomenon.

Sabrefin, Sicklefin Killi
Terranatos dolichopterus
45 mm (1.75 in)
Venezuela

A very striking fish with elongated, sickle-shaped dorsal and anal fins emerging from a light-coloured, dark-speckled body. Females are much smaller, lacking the speckles and elongated fins. A substrate spawner, it may be a little difficult to keep, requiring, like most Killifishes, soft acid water to really thrive. Recently reclassified into this new genus, it was formerly known as *Austrofundulus*.

One characteristic particular to Playfair's Panchax, Pachypanchax playfairi, *is the projection of the scales from the body*

SILURIDS (Catfishes)

Like the cichlids, catfishes have an enormous following in the fishkeeping hobby. Their natural homes are in South America and Africa, with Asia again coming a poor third in the catfish population stakes.

All catfish have well-developed barbels around the mouth, and most are bottom dwelling fishes although the African species venture more into the higher water levels than most. Catfish have no scales; their bodies are either covered in overlapping bony plates or the skin is entirely naked. Some catfishes gulp atmospheric air at the water surface and extract oxygen in their hindgut. The large eel-like species in the genus *Clarias* are predators and can make short journeys overland to neighbouring waters; they are excellent escape artists too, so keep a tight fit to the aquarium hood.

Catfish are often treated as scavengers, relegated to clearing up food left by other fishes. This is quite unfair and catfishes should not be neglected in this way. Another reason why catfish often appear to be getting a bad deal is that many are nocturnal and so the hobbyist never really gets to know their ways.

Of catfish to breed in captivity, the *Corydoras* group is most successful. Fertilized eggs are carried between the female's ventral fins to a selected site where the eggs are deposited to hatch. A small number of species from other genera have spawned in captivity.

The Sabrefin, Terranatos dolichopterus, *has very long dorsal and anal fins, held well away from the body*

Individual Species

Short-bodied Catfish
Brochis splendens
65 mm (2.5 in)
Brazil, Ecuador

At first glance, a heftier form of *Corydoras* spp. (see below) but closer inspection will reveal a much longer-based dorsal fin, a deeper body and a more pointed snout. Under certain lighting conditions the sides may show a metallic-green sheen.

The Short-bodied Catfish, Brochis splendens, *is very similar in appearance to the related* Corydoras *species*

Almost the archetypal catfish, the Bronze Catfish, Corydoras aeneus, *can be found in almost everyone's aquarium*

Bronze Catfish
Corydoras aeneus
80 mm (3.25 in)
South America

An all-time aquarium favourite, this catfish is widespread throughout South America. It is now bred commercially in large numbers which thankfully eases pressure on wild stocks. Sexing *Corydoras* is a matter of observing the fish from above: males have the widest part of the body at the point of insertion of the pectoral fins, females widening further well behind this point. Spawning is a complicated affair: after hectic chasing by the male, the female continually butts the male in the ventral area until sperm is released simultaneously with a small number of eggs. The sperm may be 'inhaled' and immediately 'expelled' from the gills so that it carries to the eggs being held in the female's ventral fins. The fertilized eggs are then placed on a chosen pre-cleaned spawning site to hatch. A ready aquarium spawner, *C. aeneus* may be stimulated to spawn by the addition of cooler water to the tank. Albino forms have been cultivated by dedicated breeders but, of course, such specimens do not occur in nature.

The more recently-introduced Banded Catfish, Corydoras barbatus, *has lost no time in becoming a highly sought-after species*

Banded or Bristly Catfish
Corydoras barbatus
85 mm (3.25 in)
Brazil

The largest and smartest 'Cory' of them all. The body markings are dark patches on a gold background and may vary from locality to locality. males can be distinguished by the bristles on their cheeks and generally have much more ornate patterning. There is a light stripe running back over the head from the snout to dorsal fin. Has been bred in the aquarium.

The Peppered Catfish, Corydoras paleatus, *spawns easily in the aquarium and rivals* C. aeneus *for popularity*

Peppered Catfish
Corydoras paleatus
75 mm (3 in)
Argentina

Almost as popular as *C. aeneus*, the Peppered Catfish is also a ready breeder in the aquarium. Although it seems a strange thing to do, an albino form has also been developed.

Flag-tailed Catfish
Dianema urostriata
130 mm (5 in)
Brazil

Unmistakeable due to the striking black and white striped caudal fin. The elongated body is not quite so flattened underneath which may suggest that this catfish spends less time on the bottom than its relatives. It is certainly nocturnal, tending to hide during the day. Keeping more than one specimen is to be recommended as these fish like to be in a shoal.

The black and white stripes of the caudal fin of the Flag-tailed Catfish, Dianema urostriata, *makes it an attractive proposition for the aquarium*

The Spotted Pimelodus, Pimelodus pictus, *shows that there are other attractive catfishes available from South America*

Spotted Pimelodus, Angelica Pim
Pimelodus pictus
110 mm (4.25 in)
Peru, Colombia

With its very long barbels, spotted silver body and constant activity this fish has found many devotees. The common name, Angelica Pim, is a reference to this fish's almost *reverse* coloration to the African species, *Synodontis angelicus* (a dark fish with light spots), but another immediate visible difference is the latter's large fleshy adipose fin. Like other species within the Pimelodidae family, this is a predator and should only be kept with fishes of similar size.

Upside-down Catfish
Synodontis nigriventris
90 mm (3.5 in)
Zaire

Whilst the coloration and patterning of the body is not unlike that of *C. paleatus*, unlike most other fishes the normal shading pattern (dark on top, light underneath) is reversed. The reason for this becomes quite clear when the usual swimming position is noticed – this fish swims upside down, so the dark belly substitutes for the dark back of other fishes to camouflage the fish when viewed from above. The spines of *Synodontis* are erectile and the fish should be handled with extreme caution.

The Upside-down Catfish, Synodontis nigriventris, *is but one African species of catfish that can swim inverted as it pleases*

MISCELLANEOUS EGGLAYING SPECIES

With such a vast fish population worldwide (a list simply of those species that are 'aquarium-suitable' runs into thousands) there are species that do not fit into any of the previous categories, often because they are the sole representatives of their genus or family. The following miscellaneous species continue to find favour amongst hobbyists.

A feature of all rainbowfishes is that they have two separate dorsal fins. The Madagascar Rainbow, Bedotia geayi, is no exception to the rule

Individual Species

Madagascar Rainbow
Bedotia geayi
90 mm (3.5 in)
Madagascar

Like all the species in the Atherinidae family, the Madagascar Rainbow has two separate dorsal fins. One is plain, the larger, rear dorsal is edged in black and red similar to the anal and caudal fins. Two longitudinal dark bands appear on the flanks. The young fry (from scattered eggs) only appear to be interested in food if it is moving – live foods and aeration to create water currents will help to solve this problem.

Elephant-nose
Gnathonemus petersi
250 mm (10 in)
West Africa

This fish is interesting, apart from imagining what use the nose can be put to. In fact the 'nose' is merely an extension of the lower jaw and is used to root about for food. The dorsal and anal fins are set far back on the body and the caudal fin is deeply-forked. The fish has poor eyesight and depends on a self-generated electromagnetic field for navigation. A well-planted aquarium and dim lighting suits this species.

The extended lower jaw of the Elephant-nose, Gnathonemus petersi, *is used to locate food in the substrate*

The Butterflyfish, Pantodon buchholzi, *is the only member in its genus, which is probably most fortunate for other smaller fishes, for it is very predatory*

Butterflyfish
Pantodon buchholzi
110 mm (4.25 in)
West Africa

This predatory fish, which lurks just beneath the surface, takes its common name from its butterfly-like pectoral fins. To fully appreciate their size you must view the from above and, to prove that they are not just ornamental, the fish is known to skim over the water surface in a similar manner to the marine Flying-fishes. Breeding is slightly unusual in that the male rides on the back of the female prior to eggs being released and fertilized. It is the only species in the genus.

Celebes Rainbow
Telmatherina ladigesi
70 mm (2.75 in)
Borneo, Sulawesi

The anal and second dorsal fins of the male have long filamentous extensions. The blue-green glowing line on the yellowish body makes this fish most attractive, especially with a little sidelighting coming through the front glass. A shoaling fish, it appreciates hard water. Spawning occurs over long periods amongst bushy plants where eggs are scattered. As the parents are partial to their own eggs it may be good practice to remove egg-laden plants to a separate aquarium for hatching.

The Celebes Rainbowfish, Telmatherina ladigesi, *has in addition to two dorsal fins, long filamentous extensions to the second dorsal and anal fins*

LIVEBEARERS

Livebearing fishes may be divided into two main groups – those that have cultivated strains and those that still retain their 'wild' physical characteristics and coloration.

The origin of most livebearing fishes is Central America and the Caribbean Islands. An Asian representative is related to the marine flying fishes. Because of their appetite for mosquito larvae, many livebearing fishes such as the Guppy (*Poecilia reticulata* and *Gambusia* sp.) have been introduced into countries plagued by the malaria-carrying mosquito to help contain the spread of the disease.

Many of the cultivated forms (Guppy, Molly, Platy and Swordtail) relish some vegetable matter in their diet. Keeping the fish in hard water also appears to be beneficial, and Mollies do better still if a small amount of salt is added to the water.

All livebearers are prolific, gestation periods being around 30 days at normal aquarium temperatures. Sexing livebearing fishes is simple: most males have adapted anal fins forming a rod-shaped reproductive organ. Males from the remaining genera have the first few rays of the anal fin separated from the rest. Females have the normally fan-shaped anal fin found in most fishes. Careful handling of the gravid female is vital and she should be moved to a separate tank to give birth well before the end of her 4-week 'pregnancy'. Females of the 'cultivated' species can store sperm, enabling them to give birth to successive broods without re-mating with a male.

Individual Species

Butterfly Goodeid
Ameca splendens
75/90 mm (3/3.5 in) (m/f)
Central America

Apart from noting the difference in shape of the anal fins (the male has notch just after the first few rays), another method of sexing this species is that the male has a yellow border to the caudal fin. A characteristic of most livebearing genera is that the female is often much larger than the male. Females of the Goodeidae family cannot store sperm and require mating each time a brood is planned.

The Butterfly Goodeid, Ameca splendens, *is one of the increasing number of 'Other Species Livebearers' being kept by hobbyists specializing in these interesting fishes*

Four-eyes, Anableps anableps, *fully deserves the popular name although the eyes, which can look above and below the surface simultaneously, are merely two normal eyes each physically divided by a membrane into two halves. The fish does not have four eyes as such*

Four-eyes
Anableps anableps
250 mm (10 in)
Central America

A distinct oddity! This surface-swimming species can look above and below the water at the same time thanks to a divided iris (there are only two eyes despite the common name). A large fish which gives birth to a small number of large young. A further peculiarity of the species (along with a few other genera, i.e. *Jenynsia*, the One-sided Livebearer) is that the male's gonopodium can only be directed to one side (left or right but not both), therefore he has to seek out a female capable of accepting his attentions from that particular side. Hard water is desirable for this species and a spacious tightly-covered aquarium.

Wrestling Halfbeak
Dermogenys pusillus
65/90 mm (2.5/3.5 in) (mf)
Far East

This fish has an elongated lower jaw and a densely-planted aquarium is advisable, or at least one planted around the sides, so that the fish does not injure itself by swimming into the glass sides. Being a surface-feeder, floating foods are almost obligatory for this species would find it very difficult to feed at any other location. Although females are generally larger than the males, sexing is difficult, the male's anal fin being only slightly modified. The common name refers to males being matched in fighting contests similar to *Betta splendens*. Keep the aquarium well-covered as these fish are great jumpers.

The Wrestling Halfbeak, Dermogenys pusillus, *has a delicate, much extended, lower jaw which can suffer damage if the frightened fish swims into any obstacle in its haste*

Black Molly
Poecilia mexicana (sphenops)
70 mm (2.75 in)
Mexico

A very popular fish, whose jet-black colour makes a good contrast to the colours of the other fishes. A 'lyretail' version is another aquarium-developed strain, as is the speckled variety. Females larger.

The ever-popular Black Molly, Poecilia mexicana (sphenops)*, makes a welcome contrasting colour to the aquarium*

Opposite: The Sailfin Molly, Poecilia velifera, *regularly displays to other fishes by raising its large dorsal fin*

Guppy, Millions Fish
Poecilia reticulata
30 mm (1.25 in) (male)
Trinidad

A famous species known even to non-fishkeepers. No two males look alike and its ease of breeding has made the cultivation of colourful strains (with equally exotic finnages) very popular. International standards keep would-be 'line-breeders' on the right track. Females are almost twice as large as the male and, whilst wild-caught fishes (including males) are rather nondescipt in colour, selective breeding has also managed to inject colour into females. Introduced into other countries to control mosquito larvae.

Sailfin Molly
Poecilia velifera
100 mm (4 in)
Mexico

The main feature of this species is the large dorsal fin which is erected as the male displays to the female or threatens a rival male. The male's anal fin is fully modified into a rodlike structure making sexing easy. Apart from plenty of room, two things make keeping this fish slightly easier – the addition of a little salt to the water, and plenty of green food. Female Mollies are very sensitive towards the end of the gestation period, so move them in plenty of time to a separate well-planted tank in which to deliver their young.

The world-famous Guppy, Poecilia reticulata, *has become rightly popular due to breeding programmes resulting in very many different colour forms and finnage patterns being available for yet even further aquarium cultivation*

The Orange-tailed Goodeid, Xenotoca eiseni, *has proved to be a popular, yet different, livebearer in recent years*

The Swordtail, Xiphophorus helleri, *has, like many livebearing fishes, been aquarium developed into many internationally-recognized colour variants. This is a 'Hi-Fin Lyretail' variety*

Orange-tailed Goodeid
Xenotoca eiseni
65 mm (2.5 in)
Mexico

A pugnacious fish of slightly 'hump-backed' appearance, with vivid coloration in the male. The body is metallic blue-green offset by orange fins and reddish caudal peduncle. The dorsal fin is set well back. Only the front part of the male's anal fin modified. The females are larger and less colourful.

Swordtail
Xiphophorus helleri
100 mm (4 in)
Mexico

An aptly named fish, the caudal fin having a long extension to its bottom edge. Aquarium species much cultivated with 'high fin' and double or 'lyretail' forms; colours can be uniform or half-coloured; the 'wagtail' form has black fins. The original wild fish is greenish-silver. Males can be quarrelsome, often sparring with other, repeatedly swimming forwards and backwards with spread fins. Sex reversal is not unusual, where the female takes on male characteristics. Females lack the 'sword' and are larger than males. Very prolific with large broods, nearly 300 being the record. Several other 'swordtailed' species in the genus are popular with specialist hobbyists although the 'swords' are not developed to anywhere near the same proportions as in this species.

Platy
Xiphophorus maculatus
50 mm (2 in)
Mexico

More dumpy than the Swordtail, the Platy has also been highly cultivated to produce many colour strains, with standards similar to those for the preceding species. It will hybridize with *X. helleri* and also shares its appreciation of vegetable matter in its diet. Females may not be much longer than the males but have a deeper body.

Platy
Xiphophorus variatus
70 mm (2.75 in)
Mexico

A 'stretched' version of the preceding fish but a separate species nevertheless. Scales may be dark-edged and the most obvious difference is the elongated caudal peduncle area which may be crossed vertically by dark bars. Also known as Variatus Platy, 'Marigold' and 'Sunset' colour varieties are some favourite strains often having extra-long dorsal fins.

Below: The Variatus Platy, Xiphophorus variatus, *has a longer body than the normal Platy but nevertheless has been cultivated into several similar colour variants*

Above: The Platy, Xiphophorus maculatus, *is a stockier version of the Swordtail and lacks the 'sword'. Many colour variants have been developed*

Where Do You *Go From Here*

By the time you have reached here you will have learned the basic rudiments of fishkeeping and have maybe formed your own opinion about which direction your fishkeeping interests could take as you become more experienced. Tropical freshwater fish are, however, only a part of the fishkeeping scene. Your hobby has a long history and perhaps an even more exciting future.

Fish were first cultivated purely for food and it was only later, when humble pond fish such as Carp threw up the occasional colourful 'sport' in its offspring, that people began to appreciate a fish's beauty rather than its taste.

Tropical marine fishkeeping brings its glamour and excitement as this collection of coral reef fishes shows

OTHER FORMS OF FISHKEEPING

Coldwater fishkeeping is the oldest form of the art, with ornamental Carp being recorded in Europe as early as A.D. 970. The emergence of the Goldfish in all its ornamental forms really established fishkeeping as an international hobby. In more recent years there has been increasing interest in other coldwater fishes, particularly those from North America, which provide many equally colourful specimens for the aquarium.

With the widespread use of electricity, and the development of reliable heating equipment it was inevitable that interest in tropical fishes would come to overshadow that of coldwater fishes, especially as it became easier to import tropical fishes by air from their original homes.

However, the hobby has not stopped here either. The sea holds many exceedingly beautiful fishes, especially those living in the shallow waters of coral reefs, and these wonderful fishes are now being imported for tropical saltwater aquariums. Allied to the marine fishes is the equally exciting invertebrate life, which may be kept (with necessary care) together with the fishes or in a separate aquarium. It is now possible to recreate a miniature coral reef in your own home aquarium.

So fishkeeping has very much more to offer than just the range of fishes described in this book.

*Coldwater fishkeeping offers such attractions as the more Fancy varieties of Goldfish as Oranda (**below**), and the Bubble-Eye (**opposite, bottom**). Pool fish, such as the ornamental Koi (**opposite, top**), lend spectacular colour and additional interest to the garden pond*

ALLIED INTERESTS

You are not alone in keeping fish – a walk around your neighbourhood at night will reveal many houses with an illuminated aquarium on display. Often the beginner comes up against a problem that cannot be solved without help from another fishkeeper. The first port of call may well be the dealer but there is another, perhaps better, source of help at hand. Most towns have a fishkeeping society (the local Public Library or Town Hall usually keeps the address of the meeting place). There you will meet other people with similar interests and, apart from getting your problem quickly solved, you will find much to interest you and help you to expand your knowledge and experience.

One particularly valuable aspect of joining a fishkeeping society is often the annual show. Here you will see hundreds of fishes, all in prime condition, and it will give you the opportunity to see species otherwise only read about, and help you to decide whether they will suit your aquarium. Eventually, you may wish to show your own fish. Societies also provide many other interests throughout the year, with visiting speakers, excursions to places of interest, pond hunts, beachcombing, and social events. Breeding fishes in the aquarium has many rewards. Whilst the average hobbyist cannot depend generally on a steady income from such activity, specializing in certain varieties (or rarer species) will result in a more welcoming attitude from dealers. The breeding of endangered species will also help to conserve natural stocks. Gain a reputation for breeding quality rather than quantity.

Many fishkeepers are also photographers and, today, video makers too. If you have a suitable camera (a single lens reflex is best) you can add another dimension to fishkeeping by taking photographs of your favourite fishes, capturing spawning sequences or making up a photographic record of how you set up the tank.

Glossary

Activated carbon Filter material used to adsorb dissolved waste substances from the aquarium water.

Adipose A small extra fin, found on some fishes, between the dorsal and anal fin.

Aeration Air introduced into the aquarium to agitate the water surface.

Airline Tubing (usually plastic) through which air is fed into the aquarium.

Airpump A small electric vibrating-diaphragm device providing a continuous air supply to power filters or airstones.

Airstone A submersible porous block which produces a fine stream of air bubbles when fed with air from the airpump.

Albino Lacking pigmentation.

Algae Unicellular plants which colour the water green, or which grow over larger aquarium plants. The result of too much light.

All-glass A frameless tank made of five pieces of glass stuck together.

Anabantids Collective, slightly inaccurate name for fishes (e.g. Gouramies, Siamese Fighting Fish) equipped to breathe atmospheric air.

Anal Single keel-like fin beneath the body.

Annuals Fishes that in nature only live one year, due to their habitats drying up. Killifishes.

Artemia salina Brine Shrimp. Eggs may be hatched in salt water to provide ideal live food for young fishes.

Barbs Cosmopolitan fishes most of which have small barbels (q.v.).

Barbel Whisker-like growths at corners of mouth of some fishes especially bottom-dwelling species. (Latin: *barbus*, beard).

Biological (filter) Filtration system that uses bacteria to break down toxic nitrogenous compounds.

Brine shrimp see *Artemia*.

Cable-tidy Junction box with control switches for aquarium's electrical equipment connections.

Caudal Fin at the rear end of a fish. The tail.

Caudal peduncle Rear part of the body joining directly to the caudal fin.

Conditioning Preparing an adult pair of fish for breeding.

Cover-glass Sheet of glass placed on the tank to protect lamps from water splashes; also prevents evaporation and fish escaping.

Crown Junction of plant stem and root.

Cuttings Severed leaf or stem of plant which can be rooted for propagation.

Cyclops Freshwater crustacean used as live food.

Daphnia Freshwater crustacean used as live food.

Detritus Sediment on the bottom of the aquarium.

Dorsal fin Single fin on top of the fish.

Egglaying fishes Fishes whose eggs are fertilized and hatched outside the female's body.

Fertilization The internal or external combining of the male's sperm with the female's egg.

Filaments Fine, single-ray extensions to the fins.

Filter Device for cleaning the aquarium water.

Filter medium (-floss, -wool) Material which traps suspended matter from aquarium water passing through the filter.

Fin rot Bacterial disease of the fins.

Fins External 'limbs' of the fish used to provide propulsion or stability.

Fry The young of a fish.

Fungus A parasitic 'cotton-wool' like growth on the fish's body.

Genus Scientific term for a group of closely related species; the genus name (e.g. *Barbus*, *Hemigrammus* etc) can be regarded as a 'surname'.

Gills Respiratory organs.

Gonopodium Modified anal fin of male livebearing fishes, used in fertilization.

Gravel Commonly used to cover the aquarium base. (Also known as compost or substrate.)

Gravid Pregnant.

Grindalworm See **Worms**.

Hardness Amount of dissolved minerals in water.

Heater/Thermostat Small electrical heating element combined with a thermostat encased in watertight tube.

Hood Tank cover. Houses the lighting equipment; also known as the reflector.

Ichthyology Study of fish. (Greek: *ichthys*, fish)

Infertile Incapable of breeding; eggs not satisfactorily fertilized.

Killifish see **Annuals**.

Labyrinth (-organ, -fishes) Additional organ in some fishes allowing the breathing of atmospheric air (see Anabantids).

Lateral line Visible row of pierced scales along the fish's side through which vibrations in the water are detected by the nervous system.

Length Measured from snout to end of caudal peduncle – excludes the caudal fin.

Livebearers Fishes whose eggs are fertilized and hatched internally.

Milt Fluid containing sperm released by the male fish.

Microworms See **Worms**.

Mops Bundles of nylon wool, substituting for plants, as spawning receptables for egg-scattering fishes especially Killifishes.

Mouthbrooder (-breeder) Fish in which the fertilized eggs are incubated in the female's mouth.

Nauplius Newly-hatched stage of Brine Shrimp.

Nitrate Final compound produced by nitrifying bacteria in biological filtration.

Nitrite Intermediate compound (between ammonia and nitrate) produced in the nitrifying process.

Operculum Gill cover.

Ovipositor A small tube extended from the vent of egg-depositing species through which eggs are laid and fertilized.

Pectoral (fins) Paired fins situated immediately behind the gill cover.

Pelvic (fins) Paired fins on the bottom of the fish immediately ahead of the anal fin. Also known as the ventral fins.

pH Measurement of the acidity or alkalinity of water.

Photosynthesis Process by which plants build up food from carbon dioxide and water using energy from sunlight.

Power filter A filter operated by an electric impeller.

Quarantine The isolation of any new stock before adding it to the main aquarium to eliminate risk of introducing disease.

Rays Spines that support the fin tissues.

Rhizome A tuberous plant root.

Root Underground anchoring and feeding system of plants.

Runners Exposed rootlike plant growths that carry new plantlets.

Scales Thin bony plates that cover the fish's skin.

Scraper Any device used to remove algal growths from the glass of the tank.

Scutes Large bony platelike covering found in some Catfishes instead of scales.

Sealant Usually silicone-based adhesive. Used to bond glass panels together.

Sediment Settled rubbish (dead leaves, waste products ect.) on the aquarium floor (see **Detritus**).

Shimmying Symptoms shown by fish suffering from chilling; undulation from side to side without moving forward.

Shoal Group of fishes of the same species.

Siphon Tube used to transfer liquids from a high level to a lower level.

Spawning Breeding.

Spawning tank Separate aquarium set up where fish can breed undisturbed.

Species Scientific term for a particular type of (in this case) fish within a **genus**. Each species has a two-part latin name, the first part being the genus name and the second denoting the species – e.g. *Poecilia latipinna* (the Sailfin Molly) and *Poecilia mexicana* (the Black Molly).

Substrate See **Gravel**

Surface area Area of water surface in contact with the atmosphere.

Swim bladder Internal hydrostatic organ which allows a fish to stay at any depth in the water automatically.

Tail The **caudal** fin.

Terminal Position at extreme front end of fish. Describes mouth location in mid-water swimmers. Not upturned, not underslug.

Territory An area a fish decides to

occupy to the exclusion of others.

Test kits Measuring kits to determine **hardness**, **pH** or **nitrite** levels in water.

Thermostat Device for controlling the amount of heat to the aquarium. Often combined with the **heater** as a single unit. Modern external types have microchip circuitry.

Tropical Adjective applied to all fishes that require heated aquariums.

Tubifex Small red worms found in river mud. Used as live food.

Undergravel filter See **Biological (filter)**.

Variety A strain showing a particular colour pattern, fin development etc. in the same species.

Ventral (fins) See **Pelvic** (fins).

Water-flea See ***Daphnia***

Water-turnover Rate at which water flows through a filter (litres/hour). Use to calculate how often the aquarium water is filtered.

Wattage Measurement of electrical power, but more normally taken as an indication of a lamp's brightness.

Whiteworms See **Worms**.

White spot Common infectious parasitic disease.

Worms First-class food for fish. Include cultured micro-, grindal- and whiteworms; also earthworms from the garden.

Bibliography

Andrews, C., *A Fishkeeper's Guide to Fish Breeding*, Salamander, 1986.

Axelrod, H.R. *et al., Exotic Tropical Fishes* (Looseleaf edition) T.F.H. Publications Inc.

Axelrod, H.R. *et al., Dr. Axelrod's Mini-Atlas of Freshwater Aquarium Fishes*, T.F.H. Publications Inc., 1987.

Carrington, N., *A Fishkeeper's Guide to Maintaining a Healthy Aquarium*, Salamander Books 1986.

Dawes, J.A., *The Tropical Freshwater Aquarium*, Hamlyn, 1986.

Dawes, J.A., *A Practical Guide to Freshwater Aquarium Fishes*, Hamlyn, 1987.

Hunnam P. *et al., The Living Aquarium*, Ward Lock, 1981.

Jacobsen, N., *Aquarium Plants*, Blandford Press, 1979.

Loiselle, P.V., *The Cichlid Aquarium*, Tetra, 1985.

Mills, R.(Dick), *Illustrated Guide to Aquarium fishes*, Kingfisher Books–Ward Lock, 1981.

Mills, R.(Dick), *You & Your Aquarium*, Dorling Kindersley, 1986.

Mills, R.(Dick), *A Fishkeeper's Guide to the Tropical Aquarium*, Salamander, 1984.

Mills, R.(Dick), *A Fishkeeper's Guide to Community Fishes*, Salamander, 1984.

Muhlberg, H., *The Complete Guide to Water Plants*, E.P. Publishing, 1982.

Post, G., *Textbook of Fish Health*, (Revised Edition) T.F.H. Publications Inc., 1987.

Sands, D.D., *A Fishkeeper's Guide to African & Asian Catfishes*, Salamander, 1986.

Sands, D.D., *Catfishes of the World*, Vols. 1–5, Dunure Publications, 1983–5.

Scott, P.W., *A Fishkeeper's Guide to Livebearing Fishes*, Salamander, 1987.

Sterba, G., *The Aquarist's Encyclopedia*, Blandford Press, 1983.

van Ramshorst, J.D., *The Complete Aquarium Encyclopedia of Tropical Freshwater Fish*, Elsevier-Phaidon, 1978.

Index

Acknowledgments

Photographs

Front jacket: Bruce Coleman/Jane Burton; *Back jacket:* Bruce Coleman/Jane Burton; *Frontispiece:* Bruce Coleman/Jane Burton.

David Allison: 37 top left, 37 lower centre and bottom, 58, 62, 63, 99 top, 108 top, 112 top; *Aquarian Magazine:* 91 bottom; *Dennis Barrett:* 106 top, 107 top; *Biofotos/Heather Angel:* 8, 20, 48, 68, 70, 118; *Wilf Blundell:* 88 bottom, 112 bottom; *Ron Boardman:* 51 top, 57 top; *Allan Brown:* 52; *Bruce Coleman/Jane Burton:* 26, 31, 37 top right, upper centre left and right, 46, 49 bottom, 54 top, 64 bottom, 73 bottom, 79, 81, 82, 93, 98, 102, 113, 115, 116 bottom; *Bruce Coleman/Hans Reinhard:* 40, 89 bottom, 120; *Alan Cupit:* 87, 96 top, 117 bottom; *John Dawes:* 50 top, 121 top; *Jack English:* 89 centre; *Dick Mills:* 103 bottom; *Arend van den Nieuwenhuizen:* 34, 56–7, 59, 77, 83 bottom, 85 top, 92 bottom, 103 top, 104 top, 105 top, 106 bottom; *Klaus Paysan:* 65 top, 89 top, 101 bottom, 105 bottom; *Barry Pengilley:* 56 top, 74, 80, 94, 97, 109 bottom, 117 top; *Photo Aquatics/S. Frank:* 53 bottom, 61 bottom, 69 top, 95 top; *Photo Aquatics/R. Zukal:* 64 top, 65 bottom, 88 top, 90, 92 top; *Ann Powell:* 32 left; *Mike Sandford:* 29 bottom right, 49 top and centre, 53 top, 54 bottom, 55 top, 60, 67 bottom, 71, 73 top, 76 top, 78 bottom, 96 bottom, 107 bottom, 109 top, 111 bottom, 116 top; *David Sands:* 42, 85 bottom; *Ian Sellick:* 29 top left, 32 right, 72 top, 108 bottom; *Noreen Tan:* 121 bottom; *Bill Tomey:* 29 top right and bottom left, 33, 43, 45 top and bottom, 50 bottom, 51 bottom, 55 bottom, 61 top, 66 top and bottom, 67 top, 69 bottom, 72 bottom, 75, 76 bottom, 78 top, 83 top, 84, 86, 91 top, 95 bottom, 99 bottom, 100, 104 bottom, 110, 111 top, 114; *Wildlife Photos:* 101 top.